The New Short Course in Wine

Lynn Hoffman, Ph.D.

PEARSON

Prentice
Hall

Upper Saddle River, New Jersey 07458

Library of Congress Cataloging-in-Publication Data

Hoffman, L. F. (Lynn F.)
  The new short course in wine / Lynn Hoffman.
    p. cm.
  ISBN 0-13-118636-1
  1. Wine and wine making.   I. Title.
  TP548.H567 2007
  641.2'2--dc22

                                    2005036545

Director of Development:
  Vernon R. Anthony
Senior Editor: Eileen McClay
Assistant Editor: Ann Brunner
Editorial Assistant: Marion Gottlieb
Executive Marketing Manager:
  Ryan DeGrote
Senior Marketing Coordinator:
  Elizabeth Farrell
Marketing Assistant: Les Roberts
Director of Manufacturing and
  Production: Bruce Johnson

Managing Editor: Mary Carnis
Production Liaison: Jane Bonnell
Production Editor: Mike Remillard, Pine
  Tree Composition
Manufacturing Manager: Ilene Sanford
Manufacturing Buyer: Cathleen Petersen
Senior Design Coordinator: Miguel Ortiz
Cover Designer: Linda Punskovsky
Cover Image: PhotoAlto/eStockPhoto
Composition: Pine Tree Composition
Printer/Binder: R. R. Donnelley & Sons
  Company

Image credits appear on pages ix–x, which constitute a continuation of the copyright page.

Pearson Education LTD.
Pearson Education Singapore, Pte. Ltd.
Pearson Education Canada, Ltd.
Pearson Education–Japan

Pearson Education Australia PTY, Limited
Pearson Education North Asia Ltd.
Pearson Educación de Mexico, S.A. de C.V.
Pearson Education Malaysia, Pte. Ltd.

10 9 8 7 6 5 4 3 2 1
ISBN 0-13-118636-1

Contents

Foreword

This book is a perfect introduction to the extraordinarily rich world of wine for those who are just beginning to acquaint themselves with this magical beverage.

I am privileged to work with wine, a wondrous liquid that is utterly unique among our various drinks. While wine is, at base, a source of refreshment and a beverage to be taken with food, it uniquely among beverages carries the possibility of expressing human aesthetic sensibilities and cultural heritage. Wine can inspire us as art inspires us. Its very essence is transformation; it is created through a rather tumultuous fermentation process and continues to evolve and change throughout its life. If simple, rude grapes can be transformed into something as wondrously intricate and compelling as fine wine, perhaps we can take our own life experience and fashion ourselves into complex works of art.

There is indeed a dizzying array of wines in the market, and it is important to understand a very important distinction, which is sometimes blurred. Wine can essentially be a more or less industrial product, produced on a vast scale, massaged and manipulated for a standardized taste, from grapes that arrive at the winery in a seemingly endless stream of trucks heaped to the very brim. Wine can also be a very personal, artisanal product, which reflects a unique sense of place, or *terroir*. This is the winemaker's highest achievement, and yet we call both of these products "wine." There is a reason why the latter product may cost ten to thirty times the former that is not always obvious, except to the true vinous *cognoscenti;* this book will begin to demystify that particular. We should enjoy the simple wines if they are well made, knowing that there is a place for them, and savor the great wines with the pleasure that comes from knowledge and the knowledge that comes from pleasure.

May your growing knowledge enrich your life and give you great pleasure.

Randall Grahm

Acknowledgments

Writing is lonely business, but no one writes a book alone. Support and advice and encouragement came from: Dr. Judith Sills, Gerry Sills, Spencer Hoffman, Ginni Linn, Waltraud Moritz, Peter Nyheim, Francis McFadden, Captain Geoffrey Spaulding, Eric and Lee Miller, Peter Reed, Michelle Boyd, Barbara Young, Doug Shafer, Francis Hogan, Rodman del Castillo, John Komes, Chris Howell, J.R. Lanford, and especially Dr. Brigitte Steger.

I would like to acknowledge my reviewers: Tim Dodd, Texas Tech University; Chris Brandmeir, Highline Community College; and Anthony J. Strianese, Schenectady County Community College.

Image Credits

p. 76   Trevor Hill © Dorling Kindersley
p. 81   © Dorling Kindersley

Chapter 6
p. 86   © Dorling Kindersley
p. 88   Courtesy of Lynn Hoffman
p. 89   Courtesy of Lynn Hoffman
p. 90   Courtesy of Lynn Hoffman
p. 91   Courtesy of Lynn Hoffman
p. 92   Courtesy of Lynn Hoffman
p. 97   DK Images/Lindsey Stock

Chapter 7
p. 107   Ian O'Leary © Dorling Kindersley
p. 108   Peter Chadwick © Dorling Kindersley
p. 110   Andy Crawford © Dorling Kindersley

Chapter 8
p. 114   Ian O'Leary © Dorling Kindersley
p. 117   Photolibrary.Com

Introduction: What's Wine?

First and in the most obvious sense, wine is fermented fruit juice. **Fermentation** is the work of yeast, a tiny and **ubiquitous** one-celled organism that eats sugar and gives off **alcohol,** heat and carbon dioxide in the process.

In a sugary solution, yeast will continue this useful work until the sugar is all used up or the alcohol content of the solution reaches a point where the yeast becomes inactive. For most wild yeasts, that point is at 4 or 5 percent alcohol. A properly bred wine yeast, on the other hand, will continue its useful labor until an alcohol level of at least 12 percent is reached.

It's worth noting that one gram of sugar "ferments out" to provide approximately half a gram of alcohol. That means that if you measure the amount of sugar in the grape juice, you know the amount of alcohol that you'll have in your wine. More importantly, if you know how much alcohol you want in your wine, you can pick the grapes when they have developed the right amount of sugar.

Almost any sugary solution will support fermentation, and it seems that just about every possible sweet liquid has been fermented from time to time. An amateur winemaker's guide in my library lists recipes for the production of wines from almonds, apples, bananas, barley, beetroot, birch sap, cloves, clover, eggplant, guava, lemons, oak leaves, orange juice, parsley, parsnips, peapods, squash, tea, tomatoes, wallflowers, yarrow, and yes, to complete the alphabet, zinnias.

Unfortunate souls deprived of wine by virtue of **Prohibition,** imprisonment, or military service have made tasty wines from raisins, table sugar, and tea. In fact, with the addition of the proper nutrients for the yeast (which can be purchased at any winemakers' supply), there's a whole world of fermentable possibilities out there. We could make wine from flat cola, pancake syrup, fruit punch, or crushed and macerated breakfast cereal. In fact, fermentation is so close to inevitable that most of these products contain chemicals called "preservatives" whose sole purpose is to make them inhospitable to yeasts and therefore unfermentable.

We could make all these different wines, but we don't. With a few exceptions, such as cider made from apples, perry from pears, and mead from honey, we make wine from grapes and grapes alone. In fact, we restrict our winemaking to a handful of **varieties** of grapes. Why? First of all, grapes are marvelously convenient for the purpose. When they're ripe, grapes reach a concentration of sugar that is high enough to supply the yeast with food enough to make 10 to 15 percent alcohol from their juice. The native **acid** in grapes, tartaric acid, is a good weapon against bacterial spoilage so grape wine will last longer than wines made from other fruit. Grape juice also makes a naturally clear wine with no **pectin** from the fruit's skin to cloud it. Grapes can be grown in almost any temperate location and can be cultivated to give staggering amounts of fruit per acre.

> Compound wines, made from grapes and other fruit and flavors, used to be more common. It wasn't until 1907 that France enacted a law defining wine as a drink made from grapes and grape juice only.

Grape vines have another advantage. They have an incredible tendency to variability. (Wheat, that other pillar of Mediterranean civilization, has the same tendency.) This expresses itself in two ways. The first is that if cuttings of a vine are taken and transplanted in several locations, each having different growing conditions, each young vine will adapt itself and its habits to the new environment. This "cloning" of vines accounts for a great deal of the spread of wine varieties from one place to another, and the change in form and habit explains why there is so much confusion over whether one named variety is related to another.

> The mapping of DNA will, no doubt, undo a lot of the confusion about the ancestry of various grape varieties. Recently it was established that the mysterious and elegant Zinfandel is genetically identical to Primitivo from Apulia in Italy and that both of them are descended from a common Croatian ancestor.

This kind of variability doesn't involve genetic change. It's simply a matter of a different expression in each environment of the vine's genetic potential. But grapes also have a remarkable tendency to develop spontaneous genetic mutations, or bud sports. A vine that usually produces small berries may all of a sudden produce a bud whose berries are huge. The black-fruited Gamay vine sometimes produces branches with white grapes. Seedless table grapes are also the result of such a bud sport. This is true genetic change, and the resultant growth can itself be **cloned**, producing a new variety.

We can only wonder what these sudden appearances of strange new fruit from an established vine must have seemed like to early cultivators. They must have thought the vine and its wine to be godlike and benevolent. If they did, it is an opinion that has been shared over the centuries by many vintners and not a few writers.

Vines are generous, too. Even old vines severely pruned to concentrate their juice will produce over a thousand full-sized bottles per acre. Irrigation and lenient pruning can multiply that figure ten-fold. That's more than 800 cases of wine from an area as long as a football field and 121 feet wide.

Most importantly, the fermented juice of grapes is delicious. At its most common, it's a fresh and fruity drink that quenches the thirst and gladdens the heart. At its most exalted, the basic flavors of the grape are transformed by fermentation and aging into a symphony of aromas and tastes and lingering associations. People are enthusiastic about wine because it has so much to offer the senses.

The Taste of Wine

There are three main sources of flavor in wine.

- The grape variety.
- The place where it is grown.
- The winemaking techniques used.

You could argue for any of these as the primary source of wine's flavor and could easily produce pairs of wines that support your claim.

Grape varieties, like apple varieties, have different flavors. These differences become accentuated when grape juice (called *must* in the trade) ferments into wine and produces or reveals its unique set of acids, **esters,** and other flavor chemicals.

Vineyards have their own flavors, too. Apart from obvious considerations like sun exposure and soil structure, we know depressingly little about how this works. People who own the vineyards that produce the best wines often make a great deal of the unique contribution of their particular patch of ground, and we can hardly blame them.

"Them" in this case is mostly the French, who use the word *terroir* to express this influence. Many of these winemakers consider their mission to be allowing their wine to "express the nature of the **terroir**." Incidentally, all the possible jokes about "terroirists" have already been made.

Winemaking techniques expand, contract, or radically alter the taste of wine. Some of these alterations—like prolonged contact between the freshly crushed juice and the grape skins or the choice of yeast—are in deliberate service to the flavors they produce. Others, like filtration and **pasteurization,** are driven by economic considerations and have secondary—and sometimes unfortunate—flavor consequences.

The Question of Sulfites/Sulfates

If you have read any good wine labels lately, you may have noticed this caution-ary note: "Warning! Contains Sulfites." Since the Food and Drug Administration began requiring this label, there has been some concern and a lot of questions. People wonder when "they" started adding sulfites to the wine. They ask if the sulfites are like pesticides and wonder if sulfites will hurt them.

The answers to those questions are: since Roman times, no, and not likely. Sulphur matches have been burned inside wine casks for over two thousand years. The sulphur dioxide gas that is produced prevents vinegar from forming in the wine residue in the barrel and contaminating the next vintage. Today, a solution of potassium metabisulfate serves the same purpose. This chemical is also used to clean winemaking equipment, and small amounts may be added to the freshly crushed grapes to kill off any wild yeast that has grown on the grape skins or settled into the juice. (Grape juice contains a small proportion of sul-fates naturally.)

Sulfur is occasionally used on the surface of grapes, but its use there is no more toxic than at any other time. The warning label is attached to wine these days only because some very few people, mostly asthmatics, experience a bad reaction to sulfites. If you think that you may be sensitive to sulfites, you should consider avoiding other food products besides wine. Most wines have between 25 and 80 parts per million (ppm) of sulfite: Fresh salsa can contain 1500 ppm and precut french fried potatoes as much as 1000 ppm. Dried golden raisins and dried apricots can easily reach 1000 ppm.

How Do You Learn about Wine?

If the wine industry is huge—33 billion bottles a year worldwide—then the wine education industry isn't far behind. Almost every major newspaper in the coun-try employs a wine writer. There are magazines devoted entirely to wine and clubs, guilds, and societies that get together to celebrate it. A recent trip to a bookstore revealed almost eight feet of shelf space devoted to books about wine.

In fact, the subject itself is huge. Simply keeping track of all the names can be daunting, and it sometimes seems that wine lovers are speaking their own language and living in their own world with its own cast of characters.

Maybe you should take a clue from the anthropologists, those misfitty folks who leave their homelands, learn a new language, and become acquainted with a whole host of new characters. What they do is throw themselves into the middle of things and start everywhere at once. Participant observation, they call it, and it's a good idea.

Let's start participating by making some cider.

Apple cider is North America's original drink. You see, when the Pilgrims first landed in Massachusetts, they were shocked to find that the barley that they needed for their customary beer would not grow in the harsh New England winter. Sharing the European aversion to water, they planted apple trees and crushed the fruit for juice. The juice obligingly transformed itself into the mildly alcoholic cider, and within a few years, cider consumption had reached gargantuan proportions. Because people of all ages drank it—and it was served all day from breakfast on—there must have been a pleasant buzz abroad in the land.

To make cider, buy a gallon of apple juice with no preservatives. (The preservatives are there to keep it from turning into cider.) If you can't find that, get a gallon jug and put in two 12-ounce cans of apple juice concentrate and 96 ounces of water. You'll also need a small package of yeast and a balloon. Remove the cap from the juice bottle and pour off about a cup of juice and drink it. Pay attention to the complexity of the aroma and the sweetness. You've just made room for the bubbling and foaming of fermentation. Open one of the yeast packages—they're sold by the threes—and add it to the jug. Now take the balloon and stretch it over the mouth of the jug and set the whole thing in a cool spot.

In a day or so, you'll see bubbles rising and the balloon expanding. Good. That's from the gas created by fermentation. If it looks like the balloon is about to pop, ease it off, let the gas escape, and replace it. You may have to do this several times. In a few days, the bubbles will slow down.

Move the jug to a cold place—a refrigerator or back porch. In another day, the fermentation will stop and the last little bit of gas will be dissolved in the cider. You can remove the balloon and start pouring your cider.

Of course, there are variations and upgrades. You can add sugar to the juice or pour off another 12 ounces and add cranberry juice concentrate or honey. You can add a teabag to give some astringency and the juice of a lemon for a little bite. Some people throw in a handful of raisins and get a more winey cider.

What do you notice about the taste? Does it resemble the glass of juice that you drank before you added the yeast? Chances are that you can detect a resemblance, mostly in the bouquet. The yeast has probably added something that smells like a bakery, but underneath that (if you used fresh juice), there's the fresh-crushed apple aroma. You may notice some other smells, too: the sharpness of alcohol, a hint of spiciness.

Stainless steel fermenting tanks

Now taste. Do you remember how sweet the juice was when you began? The sugar is all, or mostly, gone, and the sweetness has disappeared with it. The sugar made the juice almost syrupy, so you won't be surprised to note that this new cider feels thinner, more watery. In wine talk, we call this sensation of thickness *body.* The juice had a "full" body because of the sugar dissolved in it: The cider has a "lighter" one.

Pay attention to the taste that stays in your mouth after you swallow; it's called the *finish.* Does it resemble the taste that you noticed when you first put the wine in your mouth? Is it a long finish—one that lingers—or a short one that disappears in a few seconds?

You have just become a winemaker. More importantly, you have done a bit of careful tasting, and learning how to taste is one of your most reliable avenues into the world of wine.

Of course, you probably have an intuition that there's a great deal more to it than this. If you have ever stood in a wine shop with your eyes glazed over at the sight of 8,000 labels or stared hopelessly at a wine list, you know that there are a lot of names and words. Listening to wine lovers talk can be a little bit like listening to a foreign language.

In fact, you can learn about wine in much the same way that you learned your native language: You start in the middle, any middle at all. You master what's in front of you, and then you move on to something else. Don't worry, lawyers learn the law this way and have much less fun in the process than you will.

If you want to conduct your own parallel course in wine while you take this one, try this. Pick one particular kind of wine—California old-vines Zinfandel, for instance, or Napa Valley Chardonnay—and start tasting. Try to always have at least two different wines in glasses in front of you. Recruit your friends. Notice the small differences between one winemaker's version and another. Read up on your specialty, ask advice, use the Internet. In a month or two, you will know as much about your new friend as most experienced winetasters do. Then move on.

Remember that the cast of characters changes every year. Each new harvest or vintage has its own characteristics. That means that we all start out even every year so you can be on an equal footing with the masters. And just when you start to get smug, everything changes and you have to start again.

You can also find wine tastings to attend, many of them decidedly informal and not at all intimidating. A lot of wine tastings these days remind you of the county fair. For a fee that can range from $10 to $100, you get a glass and enter the midway, where a few dozen wine distributors stand in their booths barking at the crowd of liquor store owners, writers, collectors, and enthusiastic amateurs. On the tables in front of the vendors are bottles of wine and preprinted sheaves of tasting notes (in case you want someone else to tell you what you tasted).

Everybody's willing to pour you a glass, and everybody wants to talk. Like the county fair, it's fun. There's the energy of people primed to sell, there's the excitement of people out to taste ten or fifteen wines, and of course, there's all that wine.

The only problem is that you can't really taste the wine. Imagine going to a concert that consisted of twenty bands all playing simultaneously. What could you hear? You might, in desperation, pick out an oboe here and a pedal steel there, but you certainly wouldn't be hearing music the way it was intended to be heard.

There are other ways. Some few restaurants will make for you what they call a degustation dinner. Each course is designed to go with a particular wine. Slowly, slowly, wine and food, each wine the way it was intended to be presented.

It may sound confusing and frustrating to learn about wine, but among the many people I know who endure this frustration, I hear very few complaints.

Glossary

acid A naturally occurring compound having a sour taste and capable of neutralizing an alkali. Fermented grapes produce a variety of acids and wine generally is about ½% acid by weight.

alcohol (specifically ethyl alcohol) A colorless, flammable liquid with a faintly sweet taste that is produced by the fermentation of sugars.

Body   The feeling of thickness that a wine has in your mouth. Thick- or full-bodied wines may remind you of the feeling of cream. Light- or thin-bodied wines feel more like water. Remember, in wine the sensation of body comes from alcohol, the solids dissolved or suspended in the wine and the unfermented sugar (if any).

clone   When wine people talk about a clone, they're usually referring to a population of plants that have all been reproduced from a single individual. These clones are selected by growers for their ability to make better wine in a particular vineyard.

esters   Chemicals formed by the reaction between the newly developing alcohol and the natural acids in grape juice. There are dozens of esters that appear in wine and they are a main source of flavor and aroma.

fermentation   In this book, it mostly refers to sugar in grape juice being consumed by yeast, producing alcohol, heat, and carbon dioxide. Also called alcoholic fermentation to distinguish it from malolactic fermentation.

finish   The sensation a wine leaves in your mouth after you've swallowed it.

pasteurization   The heating of wine to kill most bacteria and yeast. Pasteurized wines are more stable, but there's a lot of flavor lost in the process. Usually only done to the cheapest wines.

pectin   A gummy carbohydrate found in fruits, particularly in their skins. It accounts for the cloudy nature of most fruit juices and is used to make jellies.

terroir   All of the factors, soil, topography, and climate that make one place different from another. European winemakers who have vineyards that make great wine often credit their particular 'terroir.'

ubiquitous   Present everywhere. Of course, this 'everywhere' is used in a special sense. If something were truly everywhere, then there would be nothing else in the universe. And that's not true, even of yeast.

varieties   Named, genetically distinct populations of grape vines: Barbera, Blaufrankisch, Brunello, etc.

Chapter 1

Why Study Wine?

When you finish this chapter, you will:

- *Have the beginning of an idea of how wine and civilization are related.*
- *Understand something of the role of wine in a cultured life.*
- *Be able to justify wine as a legitimate field of study.*
- *Understand the relationship between wine and religion.*

Does Your Mother Know?

When you decided to take a college course called "Wine and Beer," did you tell your parents? If you did, how did they handle it? They may have been thinking that you had studied enough wine and beer already in college, or maybe they were hoping that you would invest those three credits in something like history, science, or business.

If you own up to taking the course and you're questioned about it closely, you can claim that in learning about wine, you're studying history, **anthropology**, science, and business all at once. You can also claim to be dipping in to sociology, religion, marketing, and international relations and, assuming you're on a roll now, you can point out that there's even a little bit of finishing school thrown in.

To bolster your argument and confirm your sense of legitimacy, let's consider two aspects of the study of wine:

- Wine as a thing in itself—a physical and cultural object in the world
- Wine as a subject for an ongoing personal encounter

Wine as a Thing

If you never in life tasted a mouthful of wine, you might still want to know about it in order to understand something about Western civilization. For instance, from before biblical times until the seventeenth century, most adults in the Western world drank some alcoholic beverage from the moment they woke up until they went to sleep. Life spans were short and society patriarchal, so most of the business of the world was done by young men. Does the fact that medieval Europe, for instance, was run mostly by adolescent males who were at least lightly poached in alcohol suggest anything about world history to you? Does it help you understand the **Crusades? The Hundred Years War? Soccer riots?**

What did wine mean in the ancient world? It's only a slight exaggeration to say that wine, along with beer, made civilized life possible. Consider the development of farming and food production. When people first became dependent on cultivation for food, a chain of events was set in motion. Larger concentrations of increasingly sedentary people developed new institutions to govern and protect themselves. Because a farmer, unlike a hunter, produced more food than he and his family consumed, some of his fellows were freed from food-producing to pursue other specialties. The good potmaker became the potter, and the inept but robust farmer became the watchman who guarded the fields.

Medieval brewer

Religious (priests) and political specialists (kings) developed, too. Blind and lame children could be supported, rather than abandoned, and intellectual and artistic roles became available to play just as there were people to play them.

Kings and priests led to taxes and records, which in turn led to writing and mathematics and, of course, to scribes and accountants and calendars and social hierarchies. The earliest evidence we have of written records are documents involving grain transactions.

To be sure, there were some disadvantages as well. Farming represented a peculiar case of putting all one's nutritional eggs in one basket. A group that depended on the usually reliable grain crop could be devastated by a single year's crop failure. Furthermore, grain, while nutritious, is hardly a complete food. Unlike the protein in meat, grain lacks certain amino acids that we humans must have and cannot make in our own bodies.

Before the dependence on cultivated grain could be complete, three more innovations were required. One was the cultivation of a legume, a bean whose protein complemented that in the grain. The second was the domestication of animals and the abandonment of hunting. Hunting and farming are not entirely compatible activities, and the increasingly complex social organization of farmers made the center-fleeing activity of hunters less desirable. At the same time, a grain diet needed supplementation with animal protein, which led to a rapid domestication of appropriate species.

The third part of this grand transition was keeping this new, stay-at-home population from poisoning its water supply with its own waste products. Human waste leaches into the ground water, and latrines contaminate wells with enteric bacteria. A sick individual infects the rest of the group by dosing their water with pathogens in his or her feces and urine. A concentrated population becomes vulnerable to epidemic.

The brewing of beer accelerated the last two changes. Water mashing of beer takes place at sterilizing temperatures; the beer supply can be safe even when the water it is made from is not. Furthermore, the pleasant intoxication and elation that beer provided may have been more of an incentive to settle down than the dull steadiness of bread. It should be no surprise that ex-hunters like a beer or two.

Wine, when diluted in water to the strength of beer, would have served a similar function. Grapes and wine are part of all the early Indo-European civilizations. Even in Mesopotamia, whose floodplain isn't suitable for vineyards, wine was imported from the foothills of the Zagros and Taurus Mountains. The trade may be 6,000 years old.

The Ancient Hebrews, escaping from Egypt about 3,300 years ago, left a country with a well-developed system of vintages and named vineyards. Winemaking was at least 2,500 years old at the time of the exodus. The Hebrews made their way to a land where wine had been established for even longer. It is

A family celebrates Passover

not a historical accident that then, as now, no Jewish **sacrament** is concluded without wine.

The Hebrew love of wine extended to the vineyards themselves, which may have been pleasure gardens, as well as mere plantations.

> Come, my beloved
> Let us go into the open:
> . . .
> Let us go up early to the vineyards:
> Let us see if the vine has flowered,
> If its blossoms have opened . . .
> There I will give my love to you.
> At our doors are all the choice fruits:
> Both (the) freshly picked and long stored
> (that) I have kept, my beloved, for you.
>
> —The Song of Songs VII, 11 ff.

By Homer's time, wine was one of the main agricultural products of Greece as well as its economic mainstay. The shield of the hero Achilles depicts a vineyard with the harvest in progress. Greek drama, which constitutes an important source of our literary traditions, developed as part of a celebration of Dionysus, the Wine God. This Dionysus is not, like the other Greek immortals, a testy postadolescent with some issues to work out. He is a deity with ambitions.

> Behold, God's son is come into this land
> Of Thebes, even I Dionysus, whom the brand
> Of Heaven's hot splendour lit to life, when she
> Who bore me, ... died here
> And now I come to Hellas, having taught
> All the world else my dances and my rite
> Of mysteries, to show me in men's sight
> Manifest God.

—Euripides, *The Bacchae*

The title of this play is derived from Bakkhos, another Greek name for the wine god. This name is the source of his Latin name: Bacchus. A party or parties in his honor were called Bacchanalia.

By 546 B.C.E., the cult of the wine god had become official in Athens. Dionysus, by the way, was the son of a god and a mortal woman. He is killed and rises from the dead . . . his followers drink his blood in the form of wine and are

Bacchus, God of wine

given a glimpse of paradise and reunion with him. Does any of this sound at all familiar?

Jesus of Nazareth identifies himself with the vine. The author of John 15:5 has him saying "I am the vine, and you are the branches." The religion that grew up in the centuries after his death is replete with vinous symbolism—most of it borrowed from earlier wine-loving sources.

Can you understand Western civilization without a grasp of Christianity? Not hardly. The poetry and symbolism of that religion are even less comprehensible without an understanding of wine and its role in the world from which the early Christians came.

Wine did not merely ensure the public health: It was also a vital part of the pharmacy that physicians used to treat disease. Wine was also used, in conjunction with honey, as an antiseptic in the treatment of wounds and as a medicine in itself. Hippocrates, the father of medicine in the West, prescribed it 2,500 years ago for fevers and as a diuretic and restorative.

The connection of wine and beer with health remains strong today. Drinking water is still not universally safe. (With a few exceptions, *potable* municipal water supplies did not appear until the seventeenth century. It was also that century that saw the introduction of the stimulant alternatives to alcohol: coffee, tea, and chocolate.) More importantly, many people connect the moderate

The Holy Grail

consumption of wine and beer with a healthy and civilized life. There is significant evidence that they are right.

And finally, to the dismay of Puritans everywhere, there has emerged a huge body of information suggesting that people who drink wine in moderate amounts may be healthier than those who do not drink at all.

Wine as a Subject for an Ongoing Personal Encounter

Some people like to justify their pleasures: Those hours of playing video games are really devoted to developing hand-eye coordination. Golf is good exercise. An hour at the pocket billiards table refines your judgment and cleanses your soul. Shopping for shoes? Well, what better outlet for the creative impulse? And so on. The simple fact is that pleasure is good for you: it's a vitamin for the soul. Refined pleasures are better still: they engage your brain and tend, on the whole, to become more delightful as the years go on. What is claimed for virtue is more truly said of pleasures: they are their own reward.

> "You were made for enjoyment."—John Ruskin

But maybe you haven't conquered the utilitarian instinct yet. Perhaps you need reasons to fall in love with wine or at least some justifications for having already done so. Here are a few:

- It's good for you. As discussed above, there is some evidence that people who drink moderate amounts of wine tend to be healthier than people who don't. For details, look for information on the so-called French Paradox. Don't drink too much, but for Heaven's sake, don't drink too little either.
- It focuses your awareness. Awareness, some folks say, is the very definition of quality in human life. A minute or two spent focused entirely on the aroma and taste in front of you is a dose of pure awareness, a little bit of yoga with 12 percent alcohol thrown in as a bonus.
- It gives you the opportunity to practice candor and trust yourself. You may examine your reactions to a wine in the privacy of your own mouth. You and you alone are the only one who knows what you tasted: You are the expert on yourself. Your tastes will change and your ability will sharpen, but a glass of wine is a reminder that you are the world's foremost authority on yourself.
- It's relaxing and stimulating at the same time. In moderate amounts, wine relaxes the body, stimulates the appetite, and sharpens the senses.
- You'll fall in with good companions. Aside from a handful of wine bores, wine seems to attract people who value the moment and enjoy life. Forgive me for saying this, but people who like wine tend to be more interesting companions than people who don't.

The French Paradox. In 1991, reporter Morley Safer spiced up the predictable news show *60 Minutes* with a report that he christened The French Paradox. The paradox in question was that the French live longer than Americans and suffer fewer heart attacks. This is in spite of smoking more and eating a diet that's much higher in saturated fat. The question behind the paradox was: how could these supposedly bad health habits lead to such good health outcomes?

Safer's answer, backed up by medical research, was that the French consumption of red wine had some protective beneficial effect. French per-capita consumption of wine was some eight times that of America. Prohibitionists were, and remain, outraged, but in the years since the program aired, the evidence has overwhelmingly supported the idea. It seems that a little red wine is good for you. Perhaps coincidentally, only ten percent of the French adult population is obese. The figure in America is thirty-three percent.]

Discussion Questions

- What would you say to someone who claimed you couldn't be a good Christian and wine lover?
- Isn't taking a course in wine just an excuse to get high?
- Why were people so enthusiastic about Dionysus/Bacchus 2,000 years ago? How do you think he would do now?
- What can you learn from the study of wine besides a bunch of stuff about wine?
- Is wine bad for your health? What resources would you consult to get an answer?

Glossary

anthropology   The science of everything human. As with most studies that claim to be about everything, it eventually came to be about nothing.

crusades   Any of a series of ultimately futile wars waged by infidels in the 11th thru 13th centuries in an attempt to take control of the Biblical land of Israel from the heathens.

potable   Drinkable.

sacrament   A ceremony usually involving some physical manifestation of an obligation or vow undertaken by the participant.

soccer riots   An extension of the sport of European football in which crowds of supporters of one team battle with fans of another. As recently as 1985, 39 people died in a battle at the Heysel pitch and 96 were trampled or crushed to death in riots at Hillsborough.

Chapter **2**

How to Taste: Clearing the Way

When you finish this chapter, you will:

- *Have an understanding of the difference between tasting and drinking.*
- *Understand the meaning of what you see in a wine.*
- *Know how to get the greatest aroma out of the wine in your glass.*
- *Understand the factors that make for a wine's structure and mouth feel.*
- *Have a useful vocabulary to describe what you taste.*
- *Have an inkling of the difference between great wines and ordinary ones.*
- *Begin to suspect that there is some connection between wine and the rest of life.*

Taste

Do you remember being a kid and having to take an unpleasant medicine? You probably had a few techniques to shut out the taste, such as holding your nose and gulping the stuff down as quickly as you could. Your mother may have chilled the medicine to make its vile aromas less volatile and therefore less apparent. She may have even followed the dose with a sweet drink or a cookie. Maybe you learned to distract yourself at the awful moment so your attention wouldn't have to be on the horrible taste.

Wine tasting strategies are the precise opposites of these. You will approach the process slowly, focus your attention on the aromas, and linger over the flavor. You will look for food that complements the flavor. You will hold the wine in your mouth for a few extra seconds.

You want to do everything to extract the greatest experience of flavor from the wine, so don't be in a rush to decide whether you "like" the wine. Suspend judgment for as long as you can. The minute you decide that you "like" the wine (or not), you stop noticing the wine and start paying attention to your judgment. Your evaluation gets in the way of your perception, and tasting is a game of sharpening perception.

Tasting is a lot more fun if you eliminate distractions and concentrate on the wine. You might want to banish competing aromas: no perfumes, colognes, or fruity shampoos in the air. It's also a good idea to turn the volume down on other stimuli as well. Imagine an afternoon in the shade on a deserted beach. Don't talk if you don't have to and keep other sounds down to a minimum.

See

Look at the wine in your glass. Are there sheets of liquid forming a few inches up the side of the glass and falling gently back down to the surface of the wine? Those are called **"legs"** or "tears." They occur because the alcohol evaporates from the surface of the wine, and the remaining water molecules, by virtue of a mutual attraction called surface tension, rise up to escape the alcohol solution below. If the side of the glass is clean, the water molecules—in search of their own company—climb up the side until gravity overtakes them and they cascade back down. It's a pleasant little sight, but it means nothing about the wine except that it has alcohol and is in a clean glass.

Look at the wine in your glass

Be sure to notice the color of the wine, too. Hold your glass up to the light and inspect the thin line of liquid where the wine meets the side of the glass. A purplish red suggests a young, raw wine; anything with a hint of orange is older, maybe over aged. White wines with a blush of orange may have some sweetness to them. A greenish tinge suggests a young, fresh flavor. Pomegranate red signals one grape variety; cherry and raspberry shades are signs of others.

With the glass held against a white background, try to probe the deepest color the wine has to offer. This is a moment for poetry. What do you see? Rubies? Garnets? Amber? If you don't care for jewelry, there are other, sillier metaphors: Sometimes the color of a wine is called its **"robe,"** and a richly colored wine can be said to be "well-dressed." One of the best things about attending to the color is that it slows you down and adds the spice of anticipation to your cup. Some thoughtful wine drinkers have extended this attitude to other areas of their lives and swear they have profited from it.

Your visual inspection may reveal some small crystals on the cork or the bottom of the bottle. The sediment just means that the winemaker decided not to use a filter to make a prettier wine and instead chose to make a more natural and flavorful one. The crystals are **winestone** potassium bitartarate, a natural product of the tartaric acid in the grapes. They precipitated out of the wine when the wine was chilled. The crystals and the sediment are completely harmless.

Swirl

Swirl the wine in the glass to increase evaporation and release the bouquet. Your sense of smell is, after all, excited only by airborne molecules that escape from the wine. It just takes a few escapees to do the job (some aromas can be detected at concentrations of as little as one part per trillion). When you swirl, you coat the inside of the glass with a layer of wine, and that layer releases aroma into the air as much as the wine in the bottom of the glass. If the wine is overchilled, holding the bowl of the glass in your hand or pouring it carefully into another glass can help make the aroma more available.

Sniff

Your sense of smell is a faculty located on a small patch of skin called the **olfactory epithelium**, which is located inside your skull behind your nose and at the same level as your eyes. The patch contains some 5 million receptor cells—about the same number as can be claimed by a mouse. In normal breathing, only 5 to 10 percent of inhaled air reaches this sensory receptor. You can increase the amount of stimulation at the epithelium by a factor of ten simply by using your nose to take sharp, deep sniffs before you drink. Loud nasal honkings that would be inappropriate at the dinner table are in order at a wine

Swirling wine in a glass

Sniffing wine

tasting. You'll notice that if you sniff a second time, your impression is diminished, a third attempt and you notice even less—the nose fatigues quickly. Don't decide if you like the aromas: Just try to notice and name them.

If you notice aromas—the proper wine word is **bouquet**—but can't quite place them, look at the New Taster's Checklist at the end of this chapter for some hints.

The Nobel Prize in Medicine in 2004 was awarded for the discovery of how the sense of smell really works. It seems that the olfactory patch contains about 400 different kinds of receptors, each one specific for a different molecule. These receptors pass messages along to sites in the brain called glomeruli, each one of which receives messages from only one type of receptor. All of the estimated 10,000 odors that we can smell are based on combinations of these receptors and pathways.

Sip

Swish the wine around in your mouth to get the maximum contact between it and your tongue and also to increase your sense of the bouquet. Keep the wine moving: **Taste buds** get fatigued, too. You may enjoy noticing that different sensations are detected in different parts of your mouth and tongue. Remember to notice as much as you can without deciding if you "like" the wine.

Sipping wine

This is the time to notice how the wine feels in your mouth. Do you get the astringent, drying sensation of **tannin**? The sharpness of **acid**? Perhaps the spritzy sensation of a bit of dissolved carbon dioxide reminds you a bit of soda. Notice how thick or thin the wine seems to feel. This sensation is called **body.** Thin-bodied wines feel like water or skim milk in the mouth; big-bodied wines are more like cream.

Tannin and acid are so strongly characteristic of red and white wine, respectively, that even an experienced blindfolded taster may not be able to tell white from red if these characteristics are deliberately downplayed.

With your mouth full, part your lips a little and draw some air over the wine. Gurgling sounds are permitted. You'll smell it a second time as the air brings the bouquet around to your "back smell." What's happening here is that airborne molecules reach your olfactory patch through passages in the nose, but they also get there through the mouth and rear nasal passages. Since it is stimulated with the wine in the mouth, the back smell can be more powerful and evocative and more like a true experience of flavor.

Swallow or Spit

There's a part of the sensation of wine that you can only experience by swallowing, but sometimes there's more wine to be tasted than can be comfortably or sanely drunk. At any tasting where there are more than four or five wines, you will find spittoons or spit cups.

Swallow and enjoy!

Discreet spitting is a wine taster's skill, which in itself is worth a little practice. You really don't want to blow a spray of Barolo on yourself or your fellow taster. Pull your cheeks in like a trumpet player, curl your tongue into a groove, and blow the wine out under light pressure.

Pay attention to the aftertaste, or **finish**. Does it seem like a natural extension of the flavor? Does it last for a long time?

> Some wines, by virtue of their acidity or astringency, leave your mouth watering slightly. Our mouths are designed to water when they're hungry; conversely, the act of salivating makes us hungry and reminds us of food. Other wines leave you feeling full.
>
> The first class, the appetite-makers, can be considered Old World in style. The second group, the ones that don't make you hunger for food, can be thought of as New World.
>
> In fact, there are plenty of New World–style wines being made in Europe and some few Old World wines made in the Americas and Australia-New Zealand, but the distinction between wine-for-food and wine-by-itself is still a good one.

Along with the dominant flavor of the grape variety, there will be other, lesser flavors in most wine, flavors created by the chemical reactions between the alcohol produced during fermentation and the native acids and phenols in the fruit. These secondary flavors are usually just suggestions, evocations of other tastes. Try to notice a flavor that reminds you of something else.

Aftertaste and Afterthoughts

All of this notwithstanding, the most important rule of wine tasting remains: **Avoid premature evaluation!** Linger on the process, not on the desperate rush of relief that comes from "making up your mind." Take deep breaths, concentrate on the flavors, savor the mystery over its solution. If tasting were a competitive sport, the last person to pass judgment wins.

For what it's worth, this attitude, this sense of I-haven't-decided-yet, is a another example of an attitude that you might want to adopt from wine tasting and transfer to other areas of life.

If there were a second rule, it might be to listen to other people's evaluations, but listen to them cautiously. There is a minimum level at which any one of us can detect a particular taste or aroma. This minimum, called a "threshold," varies for each person and for each substance. Since there are, by some estimates, 250 different odors possible in wine, and since thresholds can vary on the order of 10,000 to one, it follows that no two people tasting the same wine are likely to have the same experience. So ignore, for the moment, the folks around you. The thing that matters is your own experience.

The Question of Quality

What drives vineyard owners and winemakers to produce quality wines? In essence, great wines arise from the demands of a particular market. Port, sweet sherry, Champagne, and Bordeaux have all been developed and refined in response to a particular consumer. On a much less sublime level, white and pink Zinfandel, Thunderbird, Mateus, and Lambrusco were developed with particular consumers in mind.

Prejudice and Tasting Blind

Most of us don't really trust our sense of taste in the same way we trust our vision or hearing. "I saw it with my own eyes" and "Seeing is believing" have no equivalent in the world of taste. Because we are less sure, we are more easily swayed. If we know our wines, we may be influenced by a **vintner** or vineyard name. If we are less knowledgeable, the price alone can skew our judgment. Affections, national prejudices, and commercial self-interest all can introduce bias.

So, to minimize prejudice, we sometimes taste "blind," or without knowing the identity of the wine. This sounds very scientific and therefore commendable, but blind tasting is not absolute. In fact, nothing exists without some context. If the purpose of the tasting is to compare wines, it helps to know a little something like price and age or region so we know what criteria to use. (You wouldn't judge the terriers against standards meant for greyhounds, would you?) When we do comparative tasting, usually the tasters know something about the wine just to avoid judging it as something that it's not.

The best thing about tasting with others is that sometimes someone else can give you a word or a comparison that helps you identify and remember a particular smell or taste. Descriptive words help because they give us something concrete on which to pin a particular sensation. At the end of this chapter is a New Taster's Checklist. Take a copy with you when you taste and see if any of the sensations on the list are in the wine.

Putting It All Together

Tasting isn't just a matter of taking a wine apart and trying to see how many separate taste points you can discover. You pay attention to individual tastes because all together, they make up the impression of the wine. The situation is not unlike that of the careful listener at an orchestral concert. Attending to separate instruments, the concert-goer nonetheless is experiencing the total harmony of all the sounds, and that, after all, is what the composer had in mind.

So at the end, after the last taste has reverberated its way off your tongue, you're going to try to grasp the big picture, to "understand" the wine. It may be helpful to think of wine's harmony in three dimensions:

- Begin with the structure of the wine: its sweetness, **astringency**, alcohol, acidity, and texture in the mouth. This is an easy place to start because these characteristics are easy to notice.

In the case of red wines, **structural harmony** comes from a balance between the soft sensations of alcohol and sugar and the hard sensations of tannin and acid. If you can distinguish at least those four sensations, you'll be more sensitive to a harmonious wine and more understanding of wines that are out of balance. A young, fresh red wine can be balanced and have a preponderance of acid over tannin. An older wine may balance its alcohol and sweetness with strong tannins and just a little acid.

> In spite of what your dictionary might say, alcohol is not tasteless, nor is it merely "pungent." A one-ounce shot of 80 proof vodka diluted in 5 or 6 ounces of water has an unmistakable sweetish taste. That sweetness comes through in wine as a counter balance to acidity.

White wines are simpler. Their tension seems to be between acid on one side of the equation and alcohol and sugar on the other. In the case of genuinely **dry** wines—those with no sugar left over after fermentation—alcohol alone accounts for the soft sensations. Wines with too little alcohol seem watery, sour, and lacking in flavor while too much can make a wine seem hot and fumy.

Taken all together, the elements of structure in a harmonious wine can make a small, subtle impression or a big, powerful one.

- What families of flavors do you notice? Does the wine mostly remind you of fruit? Of flowers? Perhaps you notice spicy, herbal, or earthy and mineral components. Does the front of your tongue detect any sweetness?

> It's easy to get confused about the nature of sweetness in wine. Certain fruity and spicy flavors—vanilla or strawberries, for instance—remind us of sweetness even in the absence of sugar. Real sweetness is detected on the very front of the tongue.

- A wine's structure should complement its flavor and bouquet. We want a big-boned wine to have a penetrating bouquet and a blockbuster flavor, and we want subtle aromas and tastes to go along with a delicate mouth feel. We sense instinctively when one of these three properties is out of proportion.

> "In weak vintage years, good vineyard wines are weak in structure."—John Komes, Proprietor, Flora Springs Winery

Does the wine smell like it tastes? Flavor and bouquet should be similar, both in intensity and character. The wine should seem like a well-balanced whole.

- Finally, consider your whole impression of the wine from first look and sniff all the way through to the finish. Imagine it like a story or a symphony with a beginning, middle, and end. Some wines may leave you with a short, peculiar little finish or be all nose, no taste. The best wines tell a good story all the way through.

> Think of the wine as a cylinder going through your palate from first sniff to finish. You want the wine to be the same size all the way through.

Vocabulary

You need words to describe all of this. The words are necessary because we can't conjure up images of smells or tastes without them. It's a lot like learning to appreciate any profound sensory or artistic experience: We stumble around trying to name what we experience only to find that the names actually help us experience more.

Understandable as the impulse to make up a vocabulary is, wine talk is still inherently weird. We don't have a lot of words to describe tastes apart from words that give examples of similar tastes. So:

"It tastes like strawberries."

"Oh? What do strawberries taste like?"

"Sort of like this."

This is perfectly circular and takes us nowhere fast, so people reach. If they don't have words for taste, maybe they can borrow another set of words, and the next thing you know, a wine is being described as "amusing in its impudence but clearly unfocused" or something almost as silly.

But people want to talk about wine, and one curious phenomenon helps them do it. The taste of wine creates for some of us a visual and physical impression. It's easy to say that a wine is "heavy" or "light," and most people will know what you mean. We also seem to understand intuitively the difference between a "big" wine and a "little" one.

A wine in balance suggests roundness, and you hear that word used a lot. You may have already tasted a wine that you found "flat." Or perhaps there wasn't much wine in your wine and you found it "thin," "stingy," or "empty." A bit more alcohol and fruit extract and you find yourself saying things like "fat" or "full" or even "generous." Tannin and acid make a wine "muscular" or "hard." Their lack and the presence of sugar and alcohol make a wine "supple" or "soft" or even "smooth." Too low a level of acidity and the wine is "flabby."

Now it's easy to see how this vocabulary of structure could, in the hands of a playful person, get extended a bit. Let your imagination run and try to imagine the wines that might be described as follows:

- "Like a Reubens' nude"

Peter Paul Rubens, "The Three Graces"

- "Frivolous"

"Spongebob Squarepants" provided by Nickelodeon

- "Vivacious"

Marilyn Monroe circa 1959

The Moral of the Story

Remember that this is a serious business but not a solemn one; you're allowed to have fun. Wine should be a gift to the spirit and not a burden on it. My experience tells me that tasting is mostly a matter of paying attention and practicing. You can practice paying attention any time you are aware of aromas. My experience also suggests that time spent sharpening your awareness of flavors—in wine or anything else—is time that's invested in heightening your awareness of the rest of the world and is time very well-spent indeed.

At the end of all your tasting, you'll probably want to say something about what you experienced. You'll want that to be a genuine reflection of you and you alone. Now quick, try to think of any other areas in life where you're allowed, much less encouraged, to experience something and tell the truth.

"Don't you love Aunt Minnie's new hat?"

"She has a natural feel for the violin, doesn't she?"

"Isn't Mom the best cook?"

"God, that was great. Was it good for you, too?"

Using the New Taster's Checklist

The New Taster's Checklist is an inventory of bouquet and flavor. To use it, first describe the mouth feel. Use the line to rate the body along a continuum from thick to thin. Ask yourself if the wine is astringent or spritzy. See if you notice any of the flavors that are in boldface type on the sheet. Make a check after that flavor. Then see if you can refine your observation. If you "get" a fruity taste, for instance, see if you can decide what kind of fruit. When you're done, you'll have a flavor profile for that wine.

You'll notice that there's no place on the checklist for a score. You may have seen scores or wine ratings touted on the shelf tags in liquor stores. These ratings come from the pages of magazines like the *Wine Spectator* and *Wine and Spirits*. Thousands of wines are tasted, described, and rated, usually on a 100-point scale. It sounds like a perfect solution, but in fact, it's only a start. First, you have to remember that these are consensus **ratings,** averages that will downgrade an eccentric wine that might be perfect for you.

Second, not all of these tastings are blind, or even particularly nearsighted, and sometimes a reputation can influence judgments. Can you taste the wine that came from a factory packed in a one-gallon jug without having a predisposition to praise it or downgrade it? Good for you if you can, but most of us are made of weaker stuff. Third, it's possible that the other tasters don't value the same things that you do. Some people are more taken with delicate floral

New Taster's Checklist

Body: Thick _____ Thin _____ Astringent _____ Spritzy _____

Fruits ____: Grape ____ Cherry ____ Citrus ____

Plum ____ Apple ____ Berry ____ Strawberry ____

Melon ____ Tropical ____ Peach _____

Dried Fruit ____: Raisin ____ Prune ____ Fig ____

Nutty ____: Almond ____ Other ____

Floral ____: Honey ____ Rose ____

Spice ____: Vanilla ____ Black Pepper ____ Licorice ____

Earthy ____: Mushroom ____ Forest Soils ____ Leather ____

Meaty ____ Coffee Grounds ____

Woody ____: Oak ____ Cedar ____ Toast ____

Fireplace ____

Stinky ____: Moldy ____ Chemical ____ Cabbage ____

Cat Box ____ Sulfur ____

Other ____: Buttery ____ Coffee ____ Caramel ____

Green Pepper ____ Grassy ____ Jammy ____ Sweet ____

Sour ____

Wine Name: _____ Vintage? Yes ____ No ____

aromas; others are only moved by an **opulent** mouth feel coupled with a big flavor. Genuinely mature tasters try to move beyond their own predispositions to consider questions of balance (see above).

> For an up-to-date selection of the best wines costing less than $US 20, check the blog at http://shortcourseinwine.blogspot.com.

Finally, there are issues of quality. Much as we try to prolong the process, eventually we need to make sense of things, give them names, attach qualities, and ascribe virtues. So tasting in the end becomes an act of judgment.

What should you consider when you finally and with great reluctance have to make a judgment about the quality of a wine you have tasted? In the end, there are two kinds of judgment involved in wine tasting. One is personal and ephemeral; the other is glacial and institutional.

Your Own Reactions

You start out in life tasting for the pure joy of it. This taste makes you happy, that taste doesn't. Then perhaps you learn to like the taste of what your friends and family like. If you're lucky, sometime after that you begin to pay attention in this methodical way. The reason that paying attention in a methodical way is lucky is that if you do it long enough, you may end up just like you started: tasting for the pure joy of it. So the silly, easy but very difficult judgment is this: Did it bring you joy?

Ultimately, as you taste, you will develop your own system. As a wine writer, you may tend to go on and on with your criticism in order to entertain your readers and fill all that space. As a wine buyer, I advocate a two-point system. Since what matters to me is if I'm willing to buy some particular wine at some particular price, I mark my tasting notes with a final "yes" or "no." If I find myself suddenly unemployed, I'll probably become much more lenient with my yeses. If Disney decides to make a movie out of this text, I'll be a lot more critical.

The Taste of the Times

Having your own opinion takes time and work. That's right—there's nothing natural about it at all. In the meantime, it's nice to know that a zillion wine tasters before you have paid thoughtful attention to the matter of quality in wine. As you learn to trust your own taste, it's nice to know that there's a consensus about what makes a good wine. The consensus is not eternal. It changes slowly with a major fashion cycle about every 200 years or so. The minor cycles, with shifts in preference for a little more or less sweet or tannin are probably twenty- to thirty-year affairs. That said, here is the grave but slowly changing wisdom of our wine-drinking ancestors:

- A wine should have a well-defined and attractive bouquet.
- The flavors should please you and be in balance with each other. There should be enough acidity to brighten the other flavors. In a red wine, there may also be some drying sensation, or "grip," from tannin in the stems and skins.
- The body, or sensation of thickness in your mouth, should be proportional to the flavor; big flavors should have a heavy body, delicate ones a thin body.
- The finish should linger in your mouth and echo the flavor of the wine. Some authors would add diamond-like clarity and pleasant color to the list, although the glacier seems to be moving away from those characteristics at its own leisurely pace.

Discussion Questions

- What can you learn about a wine by looking at it?
- When we talk about "taste," are we really talking about "smell"? Can you think of examples?
- Why swirl?
- Isn't quality just a matter of taste? Is your taste anything more than a product of your times and social circle?
- Is there anything you might learn from tasting wine that would be relevant to the rest of your life?
- What do the concepts of "balance" and "harmony" mean when applied to wine?

Glossary

acid   (from the Latin *acere*, to be sour) Sour substance that is soluble in water.

astringency   Having the property of contracting the tissues or canals of the body: puckery.

body   The feeling of thickness that a wine has in your mouth. Thick- or full-bodied wines may remind you of the feeling of cream. Light- or thin-bodied wines feel more like water. Remember, in wine, the sensation of body comes from alcohol, the solids dissolved or suspended in the wine, and the unfermented sugar (if any).

bouquet Some authorities claim that bouquet refers to that part of the wine's smell that is attributable to wine-making practices, while "aroma" means those smells that have survived intact from the grape. Current usage, however, seems to favor "bouquet" as meaning all the smells floating from the glass up to your nose.

dry Completely without sugar. Dry wines are those where all the sugar has been converted by fermentation into alcohol.

finish The taste that remains in your mouth after the wine is swallowed.

legs The name given to the streams of wine that occur when wine is swirled in a glass. The wine coats the inside of the glass and then forms itself into streams that course down the side of the glass.

olfactory epithelium The dime-sized patch of tissue in your skull where the receptors for your sense of smell are located.

opulent Rich, abundant, thickly textured.

ratings Attempts to summarize the complexity of a wine's taste and all the possible individual responses to it in a single number. For a value-based alternative to ratings, consult http://shortcourseinwine.blogspot.com.

spritzy Having a small amount of carbonation. Spritzy wines may have a pronounced bubbly mouthfeel or just a small tang. If a wine becomes less acidic after it's been opened for a few minutes, that's attributable to spritziness.

structural harmony In red wines, a balance between alcohol and sugar on one hand and tanni and acid on the other. In whites, it's simply acid balanced with sugar and alcohol.

tannins A family of soluble compounds that act as astringents and antiseptics. Found in the leaves and bark of plants, tannins are also used to cure leather and treat wounds.

vintner A person who makes or sells wine.

Chapter 3

A Word About Alcohol

When you finish this chapter, you will:

- *Have an understanding of the links between alcohol and early civilization.*
- *Understand the connection between fermented drinks and public health.*
- *Know the life story of the god of wine.*
- *Understand the basis of your own attitude about alcohol.*
- *Have a sense of why wine is called a "social beverage."*
- *Have an inkling of the difference between moderation and abstinence.*
- *Begin to suspect that there is some connection between Prohibition in the 1920s and attitudes toward wine today.*

There are two reasons that **alcohol** has been so popular for so long. The first and least obvious is that it was the only safe drink on which early civilized humankind could rely. There were simply no alternatives. A large sedentary population polluted its own streams and groundwater; deadly typhoid and cholera bacteria thrived in drinking water. Milk was unreliable and for many adults, undigestible.

Fruit juice, in the days before preservatives, was either turned to vinegar through the action of bacteria or turned itself to wine by fermenting on its own yeasts. (See Chapter 6 for a more complete discussion of fermentation.) Only beer which was brewed, and wine, which does not support any bacteria harmful to man, were safe. Tribes and cities that knew wine or beer were healthier than those that did not.

In places where the grape vines did not grow, a hot water extract of sprouted barley grains was used. The heating made the drink safer than the water from which it was made. Sprouted barley, sometimes called **malt**, contains a starch that is convertible to sugar in hot water. The sugary soup that results from soaking malt in hot water **ferments** in the presence of airborne yeast. When it does, it's called beer. This beer did not resemble too closely the beverage that we know today, but it was certainly safer to drink than water.

Of course, there are other technologies that could have possibly sanitized the water supply: boiling, with or without herbal flavoring for instance, and the ancient Indo-Europeans knew about them. The manufacture of alcoholic beverages triumphed over all of them for reasons that had nothing to do with sanitation.

Alcohol remains popular even in the face of competition from other drinks, and the reason, of course, is that alcohol in moderate doses has a mild and pleasantly intoxicating effect. Hippocrates might have recommended wine as a medicine for the body, but it was Socrates who commended its ability to . . . "lull the cares of the mind to rest and . . . pleasantly invite us to agreeable mirth." The ancients were so taken with the wonder of alcohol that they endowed wine with a god of its own. The Greeks called him Dionysus; his Roman name was Bacchus, the god of wine. There is nothing remarkable in the existence of a god of wine. The Greeks saw spirits and gods everywhere. What is astonishing is the character of wine's god. Most of the Greek gods are remote from human affairs, showing up like bill collectors to remind their devotees of missed sacrifices or dilapidated temples. They have no moral message and certainly inspire no emotion in their worshippers other than anxiety. Dionysus, on the other hand, is a very personal god. His worship is a party, not a sacrifice. He enters the body of his worshippers with the wine and lifts their spirits.

By Julius Caesar's time, Bacchus had become a savior whose worship guaranteed a life after death. His rites included a **communion meal** at which the god's flesh was eaten and his blood drunk in the form of wine. As the cult of the classical gods declined in Rome, the worship of Bacchus increased, only to go underground when the competing Christian religion was made official in the fourth century.

It's easy to understand the appeal of this giddy religion. Against the grim reality that was the common person's life in ancient Rome, alcohol must have thrown a particularly appealing and diverting light. Even in happier circumstances, alcohol lightens the spirits, soothes anxieties, and lubricates the social instincts. It makes the shy person outgoing, the sad person jolly, and the dull person witty.

"Bacchanal of the Andrians," by Titian

This effect, and wine's fortunate talent as a partner to food and feasting, make wine a very social beverage. It is this ability of alcohol to demolish inhibitions, inspire enthusiasm, and encourage sociability that lies at the heart of the beverage business. People drink in company because both the drink and the company become more pleasant in the process.

Just What Do We Mean by "Drunk"?

How much alcohol do you get with your wine? Most **table wine** contains 12 to 14 percent alcohol by volume, which means that a bottle of wine has something like 3 fluid ounces of pure alcohol and a 5-ounce glass has about two-thirds of an ounce of alcohol. By way of comparison, the typical 12-ounce serving of beer contains just over two-thirds of an ounce of alcohol and a 750 ml. bottle of 100-proof vodka has 12 ounces. A person whose blood contains more than .1 percent alcohol is considered legally drunk in most jurisdictions.

Drunkenness, or inebriation, isn't a single, simple state. Instead, it's a **continuum** of feeling, consciousness, and behavior. At one end of the scale is a light, **analgesic**, carefree feeling. At the other is a complete breakdown of mental and motor functions. In between, there are an infinite number of states: some of them pleasant, others exalted, and some purely miserable. As any bartender or cocktail waitress can tell you, a person drunk is remarkably different from that same person sober. The change is as dramatic to the person undergoing it as it is to someone observing him or her. Shy people become outgoing, timid folks become foolhardy, inhibited souls discover their **libidinous** side. Were drunkenness not so commonplace, we would be astonished by it and beg for an explanation.

> A drunk walks into a bar carrying a live chicken. The bartender says "What are you doing with that jackass?" The drunk replies, "Thass notta jackass, thass a chicken." The bartender says, "I was talking to the chicken."

How do we "explain" inebriation? A glib answer is that inebriation results from the disinhibiting effects of alcohol on the brain. Does this explain it? Unless you know a lot more physiology than most, it's just another set of words for the same thing.

We're easily duped into accepting this sort of circular thinking as an explanation because, as citizens of our own times, we have a certain faith in the material dimension of things. Our faith in material explanations is made possible by our long experience of science and its incredible utility. But before this faith came along, what kind of explanation might have occurred to people who wondered about drunkenness? Forget what you know for a minute and imagine that you're tasting wine for the first time. Remember that you live in a world with few physical comforts and a fair amount of chronic pain. What would your first experience of inebriation be like? For most people, drinking probably just lessened the daily dose of pain and made them feel good. This "feeling good" must have seemed like a surprise visit to another place, a divine place.

Now the Greeks were not much for dropping in on their gods. Remember, the Olympians were a nasty bunch, and the overall purpose of Greek religion was to satisfy them with sacrifices and keep them away. But Dionysus, the god of wine, was a different sort. When you drank wine, he entered your body—you could feel the god of wine, and he was not unlovable. Dionysus calls himself the Happy One and speaks of balance. By 546 B.C.E., the cult of the wine god had become official in Athens.

He was not entirely a warm fuzzy teddy bear either. The adjective "Dionysian" has come to modify the noun "frenzy." The Greeks made war by forming tightly massed units of men who ran at each other in a spear-thrusting bloody charge. The men in front were caught between the spears of the enemy and the press of the men at their backs. These soldiers mustered the necessary courage first by performing a bloody sacrifice on the field where battle would take place and then by eating a breakfast washed down with lots of wine. Greek festivities in honor of the god were known for their wild dancing and uninhibited behavior.

Greece died after Alexander, and the Romans inherited the bones. The spirit of Greek wine, however, inherited them. Dionysus becomes Bacchus, and he appears in murals and mosaics with a halo of leaves and sitting as an infant on his mother's knee.

Mosaic of Bacchus

Listen to his life story again: He was the son of a god and a mortal woman . . . he was killed and rose from the dead . . . his followers drank his blood in the form of wine and were given a glimpse of paradise and reunion with him.

But wait. Don't draw any straight lines yet. There is a third major player in the story of wine and civilization. The Hebrews had an elaborate ritual life, no part of which could be performed without wine. The settled life of the agriculturalist in the Promised Land of Israel is symbolized by the process of tending one's vines. The weekly Shabbat (sabbath) is sanctified by the lighting of a flame, the eating of bread, and the drinking of . . . you guessed it, wine.

Remember that there is no significant piece of Christian ritual that does not have roots in Rabbinic Judaism. Remember, too, that Christianity began in competition with these two traditions (Dionysianism and Rabbinic Judaism) at the same time that it was borrowing from them. In two senses, then, wine was a part of Christianity from the beginning, and the early Christians saw drunkenness as a form of religious competition, not sinful in itself.

Even after the triumph of Christianity, wine retained its role as the beverage of health. Medieval writers on diet considered it to be a nutrient. The Augustinian monk Thomas Aquinas advised drinking wine "usque ad hilaritatem"—up to the point of hilarity. Abstention from wine was seen as eccentric and even a bit perverse. One sixteenth-century writer described the teetotaler as "degenerate and . . . of a doggish nature, for dogges. . . . abhore wine." Centuries later, when Protestant evangelists railed against alcohol in all forms, the beverages they were reacting to were the much more potent and destructive distilled whiskies and gin.

Alcohol and Attitude

Like other milestone inventions (fire and the Sony Walkman, for instance), alcohol is not entirely a blessing. Right next to the lightened spirits and occasional hilarity of moderate drinking lies the recklessness of excessive drinking and drunkenness.

Even alcohol's manifest virtues are denied by some. Many people find the altered state of consciousness that alcohol produces to be threatening. It brings out things in themselves and other people that they would rather not have called forth. People consuming alcohol are more likely to be sexual and boisterous. They're also more likely to be aggressive or otherwise obnoxious. If you've never met an inhibition you didn't like, then the moderately disinhibiting effect of alcohol is going to be very scary. It's a short step from being repelled by one's own impulses to wishing to eradicate or at least camouflage them in others.

Since you came from a home with some feelings about this drug, there is something useful in knowing what those feelings are. After you have acknowledged the feelings, it's good to bear in mind that we Americans are crazy for driving cars, and that all those cultured European contexts are ones where people more frequently walk from place to place and where a certain unsteadiness is amusing, not deadly.

> It's hard to overstate the damage caused by drunken drivers. According to the Centers for Disease Control, over 17,000 people die in alcohol-related automobile accidents in the U.S. every year. Even though almost three-quarters of those convicted of drunk driving violations are alcoholics, it's incumbent on the rest of us to avoid mixing even moderate wine consumption and motor vehicle use.

In the United States, there is a great deal of passion attached to the subject of alcohol, and many people do not drink wine. Muslims, Hindus, and members of some Christian sects avoid all alcoholic drinks. There are also millions of people who are convinced that alcohol has caused them personal problems in the past or is doing so now. There is even a huge "**alcoholism** industry" partly made up of volunteers who are, perhaps for that reason, very passionate and vocal. This industry derives its reason for being from the perception of alcohol as a threat.

On the other hand, recent investigations have shown that people who drink wine in moderation are healthier in every sense than those who never drink or those who drink to excess. These research results have not been made widely known and have been deliberately ignored by the alcoholism industry.

There is also a curious sort of reverse snobbery about wine. Members of the American working class who are of northern European or African descent are almost entirely beer drinkers. Putting aside Italian and French immigrants, their perception is that people who drink wine are members of the middle and upper classes or are pretending to be. These people (and sometimes their upwardly mobile children) may avoid wine to demonstrate that they are "just plain folks" and not at all stuck up.

In the United States, in 2003 12.5 percent of the populaltion drank 86 percent of the wine. Incidentally, of that group of core consumers, 60 percent were women.

In the face of all this vocal, contradictory, and often very primitive passion, it is sometimes difficult for low-key sentiments like tolerance and moderation to be heard. In the matter of alcohol, as in so many other matters, these two virtues are the ones that matter. For many college students, being away from home and having virtually unlimited access to alcoholic beverages for the first time is an occasion for some pretty immoderate behavior. It doesn't help that many students have no experience of wine (or any other alcohol) as a part of a moderate enjoyment. If the only consequences of drinking too much were the occasional hangover, we could pass over college drunkenness as a mere rite of passage. But in fact, excessive drinking can lead to a lot of very unpleasant results. Unwanted pregnancy, STDs, date rape, fatal accidents, and other calamities can all be the outcome of too much alcohol.

So how do you learn moderation? The best advice I ever heard for college-age drinkers was wonderfully simple: Drink like you've been doing it all your life.

Moderation and Ambivalence

None of the dueling observations about alcohol are new, and rarely has one set of contradictory feelings overridden the other and established itself as the consensus. The Hebrews were no less conflicted than we:

> "Wine is a scoffer, strong drink a roisterer; He who is muddled by them will not grow wise."
>
> – Proverbs 20: 1

> "Give strong drink to the unfortunate and wine to those with heavy hearts."
>
> – Proverbs 31: 6

It would be possible to stack up similar pairs of epigrams from other civilizations. In most cases, after the wine lovers and the naysayers have been heard from, the "solution" that most thinkers recommend is the middle ground of moderation.

Just what is moderation anyway? It's a way to enjoy the benefits of wine drinking without becoming a victim of the costs. The Attic Greeks specified three glasses: the first for health, the second for companionship, and the third for sleep. Coincidentally, one modern standard of moderation is a 750 ml bottle of wine for two people, which also works out to three small glasses each.

Another more coarsely biological standard holds that one drink an hour is about what your liver can reduce to sugar. Anything above that goes into your blood and brain as alcohol. It's this "excess" alcohol that makes us drunk.

Prohibition, Then and Now

In the United States, the wish to maintain other people's inhibitions, coupled with a racist prejudice against wine-drinking Italians and beer-drinking Irish and Germans, led to the Volstead Act in 1919. This law made the sale and possession of alcoholic beverages illegal. It ushered in an era called Prohibition.

Prohibition was a thirteen-year period in which there was no legal beer, wine (apart from that used sacramentally or medicinally), or spirits consumed in the United States. It had profound and lasting effects on the U.S. beverage industry, and its underlying prejudice is still alive and well. Here are some of the ways that Prohibition affected the industry and the nation.

- Prohibition created an enormously profitable illegal business. Because the business was both lucrative and outside government regulation, there was violent competition for customers that resulted in a virtual monopoly in the hands of organized crime. The profits from that business funded the establishment and later expansion of criminal businesses. You might say that the Volstead Act provided the seed money for the Mafia.

- Prohibition destroyed an already established wine industry. Wineries folded all across the country: 80 percent of California vintners went out of business. Vineyards were dug up and converted to table grapes (or thick-skinned wine varieties that could be shipped east by rail for the use of home winemakers). Winemakers left the industry and turned their talents to other ends. When Prohibition ended, there was a Depression going on and most of the wineries were never reestablished.

- Prohibition changed U.S. tastes and made us a nation of whiskey drinkers. Since it is easier to traffic in small volumes of a highly concentrated illegal substance, distilled spirits became more available and more desired. Most of the distilled spirits available were clumsy counterfeits of the real things: raw and foul-smelling, they invited additions like fruit and sugar syrup. When Prohibition ended, the taste for these confected drinks remained behind and influenced the styles of wine that played a small part in the nation's drinking life in the period from the 1930s to the 1950s.

A Prohibition era poster

- Prohibition defined a legitimate and venerable pleasure as illegal and immoral. Fermented fruit became forbidden fruit. The coarse nature of the drinks that were available and the illegal nature of the places where they were consumed changed the tone of our drinking behavior. Alcohol moved from the dining room and family hearth to the speakeasy, and drinking took its place among the vices where a century earlier, it might have been considered one of the virtues. This intrusion of morality into what was formerly the matter-of-fact persists to this day. A recent discussion of a new federal tax on wine was widely discussed as a "sin tax."

When Prohibition was repealed in 1933, states were given the power to regulate sales of wine within their borders. One result was the widespread adoption of the three-tier system in which the three levels of the alcoholic beverage industry—manufacturer, wholesaler, and retailer—were strictly separated, with little or no cross-ownership or control. The thinking at the time was that vertical integration of the industry would lead to aggressive promotion of alcohol, and thus to excessive consumption. Today, the system is attacked for restricting the ability of small wineries to find a wholesaler and therefore to reach the public. It is supported by the highly lucrative wholesale segment of the industry and promoted as an effective way to tax and control sales.

Discussion Questions

- Chinese civilization never really embraced wine, and the Indian subcontinent eventually renounced it. Does this contradict the observation that the switch to agriculture required an alcoholic beverage?
- Suppose that Dionysus/Bacchus had become the official religion of the Roman Empire. How would the world be different today?
- Do you think studying wine will change your attitude about alcohol? Will you want to change other people's attitudes?
- In the United States, it's not legal to drink until the age of 21. Does this make it easier or harder to teach moderation? How would you educate your fellow students about moderation?
- In what ways is Prohibition (The War on Rum) similar to the current War on Drugs? In what ways are the two different?

Glossary

alcohol   (specifically ethyl alcohol) A colorless, flammable liquid with a faintly sweet taste that is produced by the fermentation of sugars.

alcoholism   The continued and abusive use of alcohol.

analgesic   A substance that deadens pain.

Communion   An act of ritual sharing of food and drink.

continuum   Something in which a common character is discernible and distinctions can only be made by reference to small distinctions of quantity.

ferment   To convert sugar into alcohol through the action of yeast.

malt   Germinated grain, usually barley.

Chapter 4

Standing in the Wine Shop
Trying to Make Sense of It All

When you finish this chapter, you will:

- *Understand the difference between red and white wine.*
- *Know when age helps a wine and when it hurts.*
- *Appreciate the unique position of Beaujolais.*
- *Know what makes sparkling wine sparkle.*
- *Know how and when to best serve champagne.*
- *Have a beginning of an idea about the appeal of fortified wine.*
- *Appreciate why some sweet wines are so expensive even though most sweet wines are very cheap.*
- *Understand why many great wines are very expensive.*

Now let's turn from the sensual and pharmaceutical to the crassly commercial business of buying wine. You are standing, let's say, in a well-stocked wine shop. You are staring at perhaps 8,000 different labels, and they seem, somehow, to be staring back at you. The whole thing is very intimidating. You know that wine is important, you know how to taste, and you are aware that alcohol, like fire, is a friend only if judiciously contained. None of that is the same as knowing what to bring home for dinner.

Let's reduce the confusion by sorting the wines out by type.

Red and White

Most grapes have a white flesh. Red wines are only possible if the grapes are crushed and the juice is allowed to remain in contact with red or black skins. The juice leaches the color (and a great deal of flavor) from the skins. If the juice and the skins are separated soon after crushing, the juice and the resulting wine is white, no matter what color the original grape was. **Blush** wines are made by an intermediate process; the juice is left on the grape skins just long enough to pick up a "blush" of color.

> Most blush wines are pretty awful, but the fault lies in the goal of the winegrowing and winemaking, which is usually nothing more than producing alcohol in a sugary package.

Incidentally, the "wine to gladden the hearts of men" in Psalms (Psalms 104: 15) was white or slightly blushing. Excavations in Israel of ancient wineries have unearthed shallow crushing tanks that drained into a second tank, suggesting that skins and stems sank to the bottom and the lightly tinted wine was removed for fermentation. Even the Hebrew word *tirosh* (wine) contains as one of its roots the word *rosh,* which means *new.* Red and white are more than just colors when it comes to wine. When the winemaker decides to take the flavor and the **astringent** tannins from the skins of the grape and include them in the wine, he or she is also deciding to make the flavor and the bouquet that much more complicated (see Chapter 5, Varieties).

Wine for Now and Wine for Later

"He that learns from the young, what is he like? Like one who eats unripe grapes and drinks wine directly from the wine press. And he that learns from the aged, what is he like? Like one who eats ripe grapes and drinks old wine."

—Mishnah Abot, 4,20

The preference in the ancient world is clear: Wine that has aged is to be preferred over new wine. What's not clear is how often that preference could be honored, since both technical and economic factors would have filled most wine cups with young wine.

Some wine flavors are fully developed as soon as the wine is fermented. These are usually the fresh, grapy tastes, and they will fade, not improve, if stored. Other wine flavors take years to develop to their full potential. These are the subtle aromatics and concentrated, dry fruit tastes.

Almost all of the wine that's made in the world has more of the first type of flavor than the second and does not benefit from aging. It should be consumed within a year of bottling. This has led to a new way of looking at what's on the shelf in the wine shop. There are now three kinds of wine: good wine, bad wine, and wine that's not ready to drink yet. It used to be easy to tell which was which. The ageable wines were held by the winemakers for several years and released when they were ready to drink or close to it. These wines were always several years old when they hit the shelf. Reality and the cost of money, however, are forcing most winemakers to release wines earlier than ever.

Of course, no winemaker in his or her right merchandising mind would put something on the shelf with an advisory label suggesting that this wine will be at its best three years from now. This leads to the strange situation in which the most expensive bottles of wine—the ageable ones—are the ones that would give you the least pleasure if you took them home and opened them for dinner.

The prototype of the wine made for drinking now is **nouveau** beaujolais. Nouveau is the first wine made from each year's harvest. It is released to the public in the middle of November. This is not a wine that's had much time to develop finesse or subtle flavors; indeed, it has scarcely had time to apply for a passport. It's been harvested, fermented, **centrifuged**, bottled, and shipped in little more than a month. Its release date is regulated by French law, and the winemakers have harvested the power of the press in more ways than one. Release day is marked by parties, press conferences, and trucks rumbling through the Gallic night to get the new wine to Paris. Airplanes take off for major cities of the world carrying the first legally released bottles. What used to be a small pleasure that marked a turning point in the year (like a combination of Groundhog Day and Thanksgiving) has turned into a major media event.

Almost all white wines are for short-term drinking and so are all rosés. Any blush wines that are worth drinking are worth drinking as soon as they are made. Wines for later are those red wines that are dominated in their youth by tannin and acidic tastes and the vanilla flavor of the oak in which they were first stored. The richest of them undergo a softening that blends these flavors with the grape's fruitiness and produces something extraordinary. The very best of these are the wines that all the shouting is about, the ones that command the highest prices, and the ones that people drink rarely but remember forever. They may be made from varieties like Cabernet Sauvignon, Merlot, and Nebbiolo. There are other reds that benefit from an extra year or two in the bottle to smooth over their initial harshness. Some grape varieties take well to short periods of aging: Zinfandel, Shiraz, and Merlot can stand varying amounts, but variety will not necessarily help you tell which wines are candidates for aging (cellaring). The best way to get a sense of the effect of aging is to ask a clerk or a knowledgeable friend to recommend two similar wines of different vintages and taste them side by side.

Barrels in the cave cellar at Gibbston Valley Wines in New Zealand

Still and Sparkling

We're used to the idea of drinks that fizz, and we're also used to the tank of compressed gas that makes them do it. The first **carbonated** drinks were self-carbonated, and the source of the gas was fermentation. The most famous sparkling wines are those from the Champagne district of France and are made by a rigorously controlled and labor-intensive method. The name *champagne* should, strictly speaking, apply only to them. So few of us are speaking strictly these days that the name is often used loosely for any **sparkling wine.** French law requires the strict interpretation of this rule, and after 1992, no European wine has been called champagne unless it meets the requirements of both method and location (see Chapter 6, Winemaking).

Champagne is often served at too low a temperature. Apparently, people feel that the presence of ice in a champagne bucket means that you ought to freeze the wine. In fact, any temperature under 46°F will prevent the gas from coming out of solution and forming bubbles in the glass. These bubbles are determined to emerge, however, and as soon as the super-chilled champagne warms up inside you, the gas will escape. You may find that escape embarrassing; you'll certainly find it uncomfortable. The very low temperature not only steals the sparkle but kills the taste, so try for a temperature between 50 and 56°F.

Another common error is to serve champagne in the wrong glass. The wide, saucer-like glasses (called *coupes*) that enjoyed popularity for a while may look elegant, but they encourage the wine to lose its bubbles faster and go flat. A much better vessel is the tall and relatively thin champagne flute, although almost any wine glass will do a better job than the coupe.

Champagne flute

One of champagne's charms, incidentally, is that it can be served at anytime during a meal or even before or after it—even if the meal in question is breakfast.

Some champagne terms that appear on labels demote the amount of sweetening added. *Nature* is completely dry. *Brut, extra dry, sec, demi-sec,* and *doux* represent increasing amounts of sweetness and yes, *sec* means "dry," but actually tastes quite sweet.

Some other codes that appear on a champagne label tell you about the production process:

RM (récoltant-manipulant)—The grower also makes the wine. This is the designation with the most snob appeal.

NM (négociant-manipulant)—The winemaker bought the grapes from others.

CM (coopérative de manipulation)—The wine was made by a co-op.

RC (récoltant-coopérateur)—The seller grew the grapes, but the wine was made by a co-op.

Most champagne is sold without a vintage date (**NV**), the result of blending wines from different years. Vintage-dated champagne is rarer and more expensive. *Blanc de blancs* and *blanc de noir* indicate a white wine made from white or black grapes, respectively. Look for a duskier flavor from a blanc de noir. Most champagne houses also produce a *tête de cuvee* or *cuvee prestige,* a top-of-the-line bottling. You can judge for yourself whether the extra money you would spend on one pays off in the glass or whether it's just a question of conspicuous consumption.

Other sparkling wines also have their own identities. The most important is Asti Spumante, made in the Piedmont region of Italy from the pungent Moscato grape. Cheap Spumante is indistinguishable from other cheap sparklers. Good Spumante used to be fruity, simple, and luscious. These days, it is developing into a very sophisticated and interesting drink and an economical alternative to champagne. Also from Italy is Prosecco, named for its grape variety, the best come from Valdobbiadene in bottles marked *metodo classico.*

The choice of passionate amateurs is mead, that drink of the Vikings that isn't made from grapes at all but from fermented honey. Dry sparkling mead is austere and fragrant without a trace of sweetness. It is rarely seen in retail stores but shows up in brew pubs and homebrew contests regularly. Try some; you'll understand why the Vikings conquered everything from Iceland to Sicily to Moscow.

Fortified Wines

Because fermentation stops when a particular concentration of alcohol is reached, it follows that you could stop a fermentation by adding alcohol from an outside source up to or beyond that level. Wines thus fortified with additional alcohol retain whatever grape sugar was not used up at the time of fortification and mature much more slowly than other wines. They typically have alcohol levels from 15 to 20 percent.

As with sparkling wines, there is a high end and a low end to the type. On the classy end, there are wines like port and sherry, which are fortified and aged for up to twenty years before being consumed. They develop incredible complexity in that time and are highly prized. Because their flavors are very strong, ports are usually sipped in small amounts at the end of a meal.

Port gets its character from the grape varieties used. Its intensity is a product of aging and a period of mechanically assisted maceration (the foot stomping in a shallow granite tub that you see in traditional pictures).

There are two distinctly different types of port, the type determined by the aging method used to develop the intense flavors. Aging in the semi-porous wooden barrel incorporates oxygen, reduces volume, and lightens color. Wood-aged ports are tawny brown to amber in color and have a pleasant, soft, nutlike character. Aging in glass excludes oxygen, preserves color, and accentuates earthy, fruity, and tannic qualities.

Man treading grapes

Wood-Aged Types

The term *tawny* is used strictly to apply to ports that have been aged in wood until the encroaching oxygen turns them an apple-brown. More loosely, it refers to quickly aged wines that are made from lighter grapes and occasionally fined and dosed with caramel. These sweet and boozy little wines have a dull ring to them and rightly occupy a place at the bottom end of the market.

The tawnies that people get excited about have an "indication of age" on the label. All these wines are blends of different harvest, and the "indication" is really an indication of style. Ten-year-olds tend to be raisiny; twenty-year tawnies, more nutlike; and thirty-year-olds are toasty with an occasionally acetic note.

Colheita is nominally the wine of a single vintage, aged in a cask. In practice, the wine may be "refreshed" with younger wines from time to time. Two dates usually appear on the label: the year of harvest and the year of bottling. Colheitas do not improve in the bottle.

White port is theoretically possible, occasionally bottled, rarely encountered, and to this writer, completely without merit.

Glass-Aged Types

If you would like to develop a taste for port, you can start out inexpensively with **ruby port**. This wine has a lot of young fruit tastes without the tannic "grip" that frightens port novices. Rubies frequently have proprietary names like

Six Grapes or Warrior. If you like what you taste, you can edge your way up the scale of complexity and price.

Late-bottled vintage refers to wines of a single year that are kept in vats for four to six years before bottling. Stainless steel storage prevents oxidation. Some late-bottled vintage ports are filtered and cold-stabilized and end up tasting very much like ruby ports. Others are allowed to retain more of their original character and are reminiscent of vintage ports. The best late-bottled vintage ports are ageable for ten or twelve years after the vintage.

Crusted port is a blend of wine from two or three different nonvintage harvests. The component wines are usually selected from the best vineyards, and the unfiltered wine is bottle-aged for at least three years. Crusted port often approaches vintage port in quality and represents a bargain at prices three to five times that of ruby.

A port house builds its reputation on its most expensive product, **vintage port**, a curious reversal of the process by which a champagne house builds its reputation on its least expensive wine. Wines from one year are bottled after a brief aging in tanks or casks. If the quality of the wines has been outstanding, the house has up to two years to "declare" a vintage and then proceed to carefully select the wines that will be blended to make its own vintage port. On the average, one year in three produces a crop distinguished enough to be widely declared.

Sweet and Dry

In the last few years, the pendulum of fashion has swung away from heavy, rich tastes and in the direction of the light and spare. In the process, sweet has become something of a dirty word. Sweetness is still all right in chocolates and ice cream, but it's definitely suspect in wine. It may have something to do with the image of cheap fortified wines that we just discussed or something to do with the frumpy image of old-maid aunts and stuffy men's clubs.

It is a **salutary** thing to defy fashion every once in a while, and a little defiance should become a part of your routine, more joyful than the semiannual trip to the dentist, less predictable than spring. Let me recommend such an act with an unqualified endorsement of sweet wines.

I am not speaking about the "melted lollipops" sold in the blush wine section, or the "gratuitously sweetened soda pop" that sometimes goes by the misnomer of wine cooler. I mean the rich, honeyed wines that are sipped from tiny glasses with dessert or instead of it. These are the wines with so much going on, so many layers of flavor and bouquet that you can sink down into the experience of them, almost listen to the way they taste and hear whole chords of flavor.

These are the wines that Bach would have composed, that Dante might have written. They are Willie Mays. You don't make wines like these by simply dumping some extra sugar in an already finished wine. They get their sweetness in more subtle ways. Grape juice is itself very sweet, with most wine grapes yielding a juice that's 26 to 30 percent sugar. Remember that in fermentation, yeast converts that sugar to alcohol. Most wine yeasts get tuckered out and stop working when the alcohol content of the wine reaches 13 percent or so. If there is any **residual sugar** left when this concentration of alcohol is reached, it remains behind to sweeten the wine.

The grapes for most table wines are picked when their juice contains just enough sugar to let the yeast produce its maximum of alcohol. These wines have no residual sugar, and their taste is what we call dry. Sweet or dessert wines have more sugar than the yeast can handle, and the excess stays around to delight us. One way that this excess develops is to use grape varieties that produce more sugar than yeast can ferment. In America, the most suitable grape is the muscato in both its white and black varieties, although some excellent wines are based on the riesling grape as well.

Another method is to stop the yeast before it uses up all the sugar. One way to do this is to simply add enough alcohol to immobilize the yeast when its work is about halfway done, leaving the rest of the grape sugar to sweeten the wine (see Fortified Wines on page 52). This is the way that port is made, and at its best, it produces a wine of almost seductive complexity. This method requires that the wine be aged to achieve the best effect, and that, plus the cost of the alcohol itself, makes these wines expensive.

Some grapes concentrate their own juice right on the vine, reducing their volume but increasing their percentage of sugar. These are the grapes that are attacked by *Botrytis cinerea,* the noble rot. Botrytis is just a mold that appears on the surface of some grapes in some places and some years. When it does, it draws water from the grape, leaving behind an intensely flavored concentrate. To achieve the maximum effect, each grape has to be picked at the moment when it is maximally shriveled but has not yet begun to rot. That means that skilled pickers have to be employed for a period of weeks, plucking single grapes. These botryticized wines often require a decade or more of age to reach their peak flavor. They are only slightly less expensive than going to war.

Finally, some winegrowers use the weather to concentrate the sugar. Grapes are left hanging on the vine until the weather turns cold enough to partially freeze the grape. The unfrozen portion of the juice contains most of the grape's original sugar. Sold as "Ice Wine," it is also remarkably expensive.

Sippin' Insipid

Finally, there is a class of wines that don't have much flavor at all. Here's a story:

My dinner companion and I were eating in Margate, NJ, at a restaurant on the beach with a perfect view of the ocean. She was explaining to me that the best seafood restaurants were ones where you can see and preferably hear the ocean. I had to agree.

The restaurant was a BYOB so the conversation inevitably turned to wine. "What," the lady wanted to know, "is a good wine to serve with fish?" She wasn't especially fond of wine, but she wanted to know what, as a good hostess, she should serve.

Fair enough. "But," she continued, "I don't want anything that's too strong tasting." It turns out that she wanted something that wasn't sweet but wasn't too dry either. Fruity or herbal, I wondered. She wrinkled her nose. I didn't bother to ask about mineral or oaky notes.

Then she offered me a taste of the wine she had brought to the restaurant. It was cold and slightly sour with the smallest possible flavor. (It was also rather expensive.) Did I know any more like that? Well, I was stumped. Wine geeks rarely go out seeking wines with no taste so I mumbled something polite and changed the subject.

But her question is a good one. Where's the wine for people who really don't like the taste of wine but want a moderately alcoholic beverage to go along with dinner? We're looking for wine that, like a good seafood restaurant, has to be near water.

It wasn't as easy to find as you might think. You can't call up a winemaker and ask what she's got that's insipid. Clerks in the wine shops aren't much help either. Even people who don't like wine but drink it anyway aren't too useful: They tend to forget the names on the labels.

If your mission is to avoid flavor, ask for a wine that's "light" or "refreshing." Look for wine labels that mention grape varieties like Trebbiano or Pinot Grigio (PEE-no GREE-jee-oh). Concentrate on the larger sized and lower priced bottles. You'll notice that even the lightest wines have a flavor: slightly tart, a bit pungent. They smell, you have to admit, like wine but not like any wine in particular. The word for that all-purpose wine flavor is "**vinous,**" which rhymes with "highness," or more fittingly, with "shyness." The Austrians call these "asparagus wines," the implication being that their flavors are so **otiose** that even asparagus couldn't distort them.

Ratings and Recommendations

How do you translate your general sense of things into a stategy for buying great wine? First, it helps to realize that there is a lot of great wine in that store. Your problem is picking out the best wine that goes with the food or occasion and fits your budget. You will be comforted to know that you have just reduced your choices from hundreds to dozens, but what now?

The ideal solution would be to taste everything that looked vaguely suitable and arrive at your own conclusion about which wine is best. You could ask the clerk, but you suspect that he may get a bonus for getting rid of some awful stuff that the owner was forced to buy. There is some information to be gathered from the label, but not a lot. If the wine has a geographic designation, small areas are more likely than large ones to give birth to interesting wines. Look for "Napa" rather than "California," "Chianti Rufina" rather than "Tuscany." It's always reassuring to know that someone is taking responsibility for the wine, so look for words like "Grown by," "Produced by," or "Estate bottled." In general, it's good to avoid orphan wines with words like "Vinted by," "Cellared by," or "Blended by" attaching them to an owner.

Maybe you should ask a knowledgeable friend for a recommendation. Assuming your friend's taste is at all like your own, this is a very good way to learn about wine. But suppose you had a panel of knowledgeable friends who had tasted everything in the shop and assigned them all numerical ratings.

Your panel is waiting for you in the pages of magazines like the *Wine Spectator* and *Wine and Spirits,* where thousands of wines are tasted, described, and rated, usually on a 100-point scale. It sounds like a perfect solution, but in fact, it's only a start. First, you have to remember that these are consensus ratings, averages that will downgrade an eccentric wine that might be perfect for you. Second, not all of these tastings are blind, with tasters knowing little or nothing about the wine they're tasting, and sometimes a reputation—or an advertising budget—can influence judgments. Third, it's possible that the tasters don't value the same things you do. Some people are more taken with delicate floral aromas; others are only moved by an opulent mouth feel coupled with a big flavor.

Ultimately, as you taste, you will develop your own system. Again, the most important aspect of that system should be a note to yourself about whether you'd buy that wine at that price.

Reading a Wine Label

The taste of good wine may be charming, seductive, subtle, or elusive, but there's nothing difficult about it. The confusion that some people experience really begins with the label. Just what are the winemakers trying to tell you?

If the wine is from the Americas or Australia, they are first and foremost trying to tell you what grape variety was used to make the wine. If the wine is from France or Italy, the label tells you where the wine is from. American wines have grape names; European wines have place names.

The difference is not casual. The European system implies a specialness about the land and a scarcity about the wine. The American system is more hopeful. It suggests that anybody who can get the ingredients and do the job properly can make the wine.

Both these attitudes are justified. As consumers, we have to understand that grape variety and terrain both play a part in making wine. We have to learn to

Domaine Brigitte Ponte

Mercurey

Appelation Mercurey Controlée

Produce of France

75cl
12.5% vol.

Domaine Brigitte Ponte-Mercurey

BLUE LINE INDICATED DIELINE.

Samples of wine labels.

supply the missing information by understanding, for instance, that a white Burgundy is made from Chardonnay grapes and that a California Chardonnay is at least making reference to the white wines of Burgundy.

Let's look at some labels:

A few terms beg for explanation: Mercurey is the name of a district in Burgundy. The value-wise shopper will know that it is a district whose wines don't have the cachet of the more expensive Côte D'Or. The forbidding "Appelation Mercusey Controlée" is just a way of saying that the wine is from the place (the Appelation) that's mentioned on the label—in this case Mercurey in Burgundy. Mere geography isn't enough to qualify for an **A.O.C.** Appelation wine also has to be made from permitted grapes and conform to the specific regulations under which wine is grown and made in that district. What is this wine called? It's a Mercurey.

This American label makes a geographic claim, too, but the more important claim is "Cabernet Sauvignon." Very few American wine lovers could tell you with any accuracy just where the North Coast is, but every one of them is familiar with the rich, berry taste of Cab. Any wine bottled in 1983 or later must contain at least 75 percent of the named variety. Blended wines don't have to reveal their varietal composition, but the better ones will probably brag about it on the back label.

What is this wine called? A Cabernet Sauvignon.

By the way, all wine labels in the United States have to be approved by the Alcohol and Tobacco Tax and Trade Bureau (TTB), which is particularly vigorous in denying labels that use history, sex, or health claims to present their wine.

Reading a Wine Bottle

The first wine containers that we have record of are ceramic, made of a porous earthenware and, to our modern eye, curiously shaped. One of them is called an amphora; two are amphorae. The shape goes back at least to the fourth millennium B.C.E. and the ruins of Godin Tepe in Iran. The amphora drawn here is taken from a Greek shipwreck off the coast of southern France in the second century B.C.E. It would have contained about three modern cases of wine.

Note the pointed bottom. This was a jar meant to be stored in a hole in a counter or in sand. The point could serve as a pivot for pouring. Some amphorae were coated on the inside with a thick tar called "pitch" to eliminate evaporation: Pitch is derived from pine tar and probably contributed a distinctive flavor to the wine. When coated and fitted with a cloth-wrapped plug, an amphora could be airtight and the wine inside could age for years.

Some Roman jars carried much of the information that appears on bottles in modern shops: vineyard, year of vintage, and name of the merchant. Amphorae were often heavier than the wine they contained, which made the cost of shipping wine especially high.

A roman amphora

It is possible that the Egyptians were making small wine casks out of palm wood by 1500 B.C.E., and there's no doubt that Armenian wine was shipped to Babylon in barrels by 500 B.C.E. The Gauls probably invented the more efficient hardwood barrel about 2000 years ago, and these began to supplant amphorae. True barrels are curved in two directions for strength and reinforced with hoops. Because they are light relative to their capacity, wooden barrels reduced the overall cost of transporting a given volume of wine.

Barrels had two other virtues. Although their seams could be made airtight, a small amount of wine would evaporate through the porous wood, and an equally small amount of air would enter. This controlled oxidation added complexity to the flavor of wine, an improvement that we honor today by aging our best wines in oak barrels. Some producers pay further homage by trickling tiny amounts of air into large holding tanks. The wineries that do this "micro-oxidizing" aren't bragging about it much, so it's hard to tell just how successful they are. The barrel's other virtue is that oak itself has a taste. As it happens, that taste is created by a chemical in the wood called vanillin. Vanillin is also the chemical that makes the dominant flavor in vanilla. Therefore, wine stored in a new wooden barrel will pick up some trace of that. If the barrel is scorched ("toasted") on the inside before the wine goes in, some other flavors are introduced. If you have ever had a big California Chardonnay with a butterscotch or caramel note, the toasted barrel was the source.

Until the sixteenth century, most retail consumers bought their wine from someone who drained it from a barrel into the consumer's pitcher. Wine that's been exposed to the air turns sour quickly. It wasn't until the invention of mass-produced bottles that it became possible for consumers to develop their own store of varied and ageable wines.

Therefore, the bottles you see are really evidence of a great leap forward in wine technology. They also give some evidence of the style of the wine inside them. Shouldered bottles of red wine contain either Bordeaux or wine made in the tannic spirit of Bordeaux.

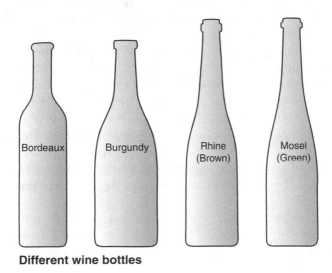

Different wine bottles

The glass is often a very dark green or gray, offering a shield against light. The soft-shouldered Burgundy bottle is likely to contain a softer, more bouquet-driven wine in lighter glass. Both of these bottles are about 12" (30 cm) tall and hold 750 ml, which is the standard retail amount. The slimmer 13" (33 cm) bottle usually holds a wine derived from a German grape. Champagne bottles are extra thick to withstand the pressure of the gas inside them.

Wines in non-standard sizes like half bottles and double bottles, or magnums, cost more per ounce because separate bottling lines have to be established.

The Price of Wine

What determines the price of wine? Of course, the price has something to do with supply and demand, and demand has a great deal to do with quality. Turned around, that means that in general, you get what you pay for. Price reflects value. There are three factors that make this so.

Scarcity

The bad news—The first is scarcity. It's sorry news in an aggressively democratic age, but there is a pyramid of wine quality with very little room at the top. A lot of people are bidding for what's available, and that drives up the price. Then there's the matter of supply and demand. There are some very wonderful wines out there, and the very best of them are in short supply. Every year, more and more people are learning about these very good wines and thus increasing the demand. Just a few years ago, the Japanese became interested in French wines, and an entire wealthy nation of 100 million consumers was added to the market. This means that some outstanding wines can command incredible prices. That's the bad news.

The taste of the wine depends on a lot more than the variety of the grape. Soil, climate, weather, and viticultural techniques play a large part. There are so many variables that wine made from the same grape variety in adjacent vineyards can be very different. Wine from the same vineyard in different years can have a just recognizable kinship. Thus, those very few vineyards that produce the best wines command the highest prices. The products of those few years that make the best wine are similarly highly valued. Even in those few blessed spots, there are vines whose age enables them to produce a richer wine and winemakers whose skills do a greater justice to their grapes.

To aggravate matters further, vines do their best work when they are rigorously pruned. In effect, that means that if you want to make a great wine, your first step is to deliberately reduce the amount of wine you can make.

Labor

The second thing that makes good wine expensive is the cost of labor. It is an inescapable fact that good wine is produced by skilled and caring workers. In the parts of the world where the best wines are made, these skilled and caring workers get decent wages, which are paid ultimately by the folks who drink their wine. In the commune of Sauternes, for example, the folks at a tiny estate called Chateau d'Yquem (dee-KEM) make a sweet wine whose integrity depends in part on each individual grape being picked at exactly the right moment. To be sure that this happens, highly skilled pickers go over the vineyard at least half a dozen times to complete the harvest.

In other, less fussy vineyards, the grapes are picked by combines that look like they were designed by NASA. They straddle the rows of vines and pick all the grapes in a single pass. In some high-volume wineries, they even de-stem and crush the grapes as they pick.

Braud harvester

Braud side-view

Braud cluster dishes

Capital

The third factor is the matter of capital and the cost of money. The wheat farmer gets paid for his crop on the day that it is harvested. In fact, he may use futures contracts to get paid for it long before harvest. The wine farmer, on the other hand, harvests the crop, processes it, and then sets it aside to age. The winemaker has built a huge, temperature-controlled underground cellar to house the crop while it comes of age. If you invested in a crop and you had to wait for four years before you got your money back, the price of the crop would have to reflect the cost of money during the wait. The winemaker is in the same position.

> Don't get out any sympathy cards for the winegrower. There is no crop that yields as great a value per acre of ground as wine grapes. In France, for example, wine grapes delivered four times the value of any other crop, and a few acres of vineyard were enough to support a peasant family.

The good news—"You pay for what you get" is the Calvinistic mantra. "You get what you pay for" is probably the perfect family motto for the Consumer Age. Both of these aphorisms are very useful because they're mostly true.

The whole truth is something like this: "You get what you pay for except when you don't." The market is not perfect. Aside from quality, there are a lot of other things that create demand. When an exuberant fellow orders a bottle of Dom Perignon for himself and his companion in a restaurant, he's not paying all that money for tiny little bubbles. He's also paying for the image that surrounds a highly prestigious product and for the way an association with that product makes him feel about himself.

Incidentally, before you condemn the fellow who is buying expensive champagne as a mindless, social-climbing twit, consider this: No one is immune to the spell of a highly regarded product. Make a list of the brand names that you use and prefer. Think it over. Working-class people feel good about prestigious brand names of clothing and cars. Middle-class people feel good about brand name addresses and investments, and upper-class people feel good about brand name consumables. Everybody's a sucker for status sometimes; the important thing is to know when it's your turn.

Just as there are wines that are overpriced because the prestige attached to their names has increased the demand for them beyond what their quality would dictate, there are wines whose relative obscurity masks a very high quality. Whenever a "new" wine region tries to make an impression on the market, it sells its best wines at prices below the going rate for comparable wines from more established regions. So there are always wonderful little disjunctions between price and value.

It's possible to find and enjoy these glitches in the usual market relationship. In fact, there's a certain heady pleasure in doing so. One of the benefits of taking a course like this one is that you become the kind of knowlegeable consumer who is most likely to discover the bargains that inevitably arise.

———— Discussion Questions ————

- If you were a winemaker and you wanted your red grapes to produce the most deeply colored wine possible, what would you do? Could you also make a white wine from those same grapes?

- When we discussed taste in Chapter 2, we used the word "fruity." What kind of winemaking preserves the fruit tastes of the grape?

- Your grandmother has a bottle of inexpensive white wine that's been carefully stored in the attic for thirty years. She knows of your interest in wine, so she invites you over to drink it with her. What do you think it would taste like?

- We discussed three factors that contribute to the cost of wine production. Do those factors apply to other consumer goods? In what ways is wine like every other thing we buy? How is it different?

- What sorts of things do you learn from reading a wine label? Which ones are direct indicators of quality?
- Wine lovers frequently talk about the "woodiness" of a particular wine. What do they mean by that and how does a grape end up tasting like a toothpick?
- If you were the marketing director of a regional wine association from some as yet unknown wine region, what would you do to promote your wines in the European and American wine markets?

Glossary

astringent   Drying, having a puckering effect on soft tissue.

blush   A distinctly American word for a pink wine made from red grapes. The pale color comes from the wine being in contact with the skins for only a short period of time.

Botrytis Cinerea   The ashy-grey fungus that can infect grapes at harvest time, also called Noble Rot. Botrytis takes moisture from the grapes which increases the concentration of sugar.

carbonated   Containing small amounts of dissolved carbon dioxide gas.

centrifuged   Spun in a tank to separate the solid from the liquid portion of new wine.

NV   Non-vintage. A wine without a declared year of vintage, possibly blended from wines of more than one year.

otiose   Weak or distant.

residual sugar (rs)   The amount of sugar left in a wine after fermentation is complete. Perfectly dry wines have no rs; small amounts contribute to the body of the wine, and, at amounts over 1%, almost everyone notices sweetness.

salutary   Favorable to good health.

sparkling wine   Nowadays, only wine from Champagne can be called by that name, so this is the common term for any wine with bubbles. Italian sparkling wines are labeled 'spumante,' Spanish ones are called 'cava.'

vinous   A vague, unspecific, wine-like character

This chapter is a glossary of wine terms, so you should study all the terms that appear in **bold.**

Chapter 5

Varieties

When you finish this chapter, you will:

- *Have an overview of the complexity of the world of wine grapes.*
- *Be familiar with the characteristics of the most important varieties.*
- *Have a handy reference to some of the more interesting minor varieties.*

There are only a few species of vines that produce grapes, and the most important one by far is *Vitis vinifera*, a native of Europe and the Middle East. Unfortunately, that one sentence is the last simple thing to be said on the matter.

Within the species, there are thousands of **varieties** (see Introduction, p. 3), each of which has the potential to make more than one kind of wine. (The word *varietal*, when applied to a wine, means that the wine was made predominantly or entirely from a single variety.) Furthermore, the adaptability of *vinifera* is so great that vines from the same variety can have vastly different potentials. Of course, the varieties have different names in different languages and sometimes even in different regional dialects of the same language.

> Whenever there's enough confusion around, you can be sure to find an aca demic discipline. In this case, it's called *ampelography*, the science of the description of wine grape varieties.

If it seems like there's a lot of room for confusion here, there is, and yet sorting out the world's wines by grape varieties remains the simplest approach to making sense of all those labels on all those shelves. This is in part because each variety does have at its core an essential set of flavors. From the winemaker's perspective, a variety also has a set of limits. For instance, a particular variety needs so many days of sunshine or a particular level of drainage.

It helps to look at varieties for cultural reasons, too. A grape like Cabernet Sauvignon is now planted all over the wine-growing world, but in every case, the people who planted it were thinking of a wine like the one produced by Cabernet in its home territory of Bordeaux. These expectations, along with the perceptions of consumers, steer Cabernet winemakers in the direction of making wines that resemble other Cabernets.

Fortunately for the student, out of all the existing varieties, only a few really matter outside of the countryside where they are raised. These are the ones that have entered world commerce in a significant way.

Along with all the subtle stuff about particular varieties, it's important to remember these two simple facts:

1. The dominant impression of all red wines is tannin—that natural astringent that thins the saliva and carries the fruit flavors to the mouth.

2. The dominant impression of all but the sweetest white wines is acidity—a crispness that's necessary for even sweet wines.

Red grapes on a vine

Red-Wine Varieties

Barbera

Barbera is the "yum-yum" grape. It's low in tannin and loaded with the taste of fruit. It seems to be impossible to dislike it or even to put down a glass once it gets in your hand. Barbera gets its structure from the play between acid and the dense concentration of fruit. It is native to northern Italy, where it is the wine that's consumed every day by the people who make those earth-shattering Barolos and Barbarescos.

Traditionally, Barbera has not been made in oak barrels (*barriques*) and yields have tended to be high. There are a few examples now that are taking the quality and barrique route and are very good, even stealing a little bit of the bouquet of a Barolo. However, the majority of Barbera is made to deliver the luscious, quaffable fruit at an affordable price. Decent versions are now made in California and Argentina.

Blaufränkisch

This is a genuine sleeper whose potential is just beginning to be recognized. At its best in the Burgenland region of Austria, it is spicy, even hot and in good years has some dense, ripe fruit as a balance. With a bit of age, Blaufränkisch develops subtlety and depth. In overripe years, it is lightened with the pinot noir-like St. Laurent and in leaner years, beefed up with Cabernet. It can benefit from a restrained use of oak.

Brunello

A clone of Sangiovese (see page 77) and grown in the district around the medieval Tuscan town of Montalcino, Brunello is another tannic monster that settles down in its old age to become a velvety, nutlike elixir with floral and spice aromas. The standard wisdom is to match Brunello di Montalcino with roasts and game, but some people have success matching it with Mozart and a good book.

Cabernet Franc

Cabernet Franc is one of the ancestors of Cabernet Sauvignon and has been subordinate to it in Bordeaux blends for years. It ripens earlier than its descendant and in cooler parts of the world, such as Bordeaux and the Loire in France. That is an important virtue. In California, where they have sunshine to burn, the light fruit and spice flavors of Cabernet Franc cannot compete against the obvious power of Cabernet Sauvignon, and so Cab Franc only shows up as a tiny component in blends.

There are some wonderful wines based solely on this grape: the elegant but obscure Loire Valley Saumur-Champigny, for instance, which has a silky, cedary bouquet, or the intensely grassy Grave del Friuli from Italy.

Cabernet Sauvignon

By now, you may have noticed a tendency on the part of some writers to describe wines with human personality terms. Wines made from Cabernet Sauvignon are sometimes called aggressive or forceful or even masculine. At their best, Cabernet-based wines have a tannic roughness that transports their flavors to the mouth. This sensation of warming and drying is one that some novice wine drinkers find difficult to like but that almost all the veteran wine lovers admire.

In fact, for many wine lovers, Cabernet is the one great red grape, the single best evidence that God is in his vineyard and all is right with the world. It's easy to understand why: Cabernet-based wines can develop incredibly powerful tastes while simultaneously maintaining delicate complexities. They vary tremendously and interestingly from one winery to another and even from year to year. In California, the grape often has strong notes of eucalyptus, bell pepper, and sandalwood flavors that are almost startling in a red wine. Cabernet is originally from the Bordeaux region in France, but you can find Cab-based wines from California, France, South America, and Australia.

Gamay

This is the grape of the Beaujolais district in Burgundy, France, and it appears in your glass in essentially three forms.

Nouveau. Years ago, I worked in a restaurant in upstate New York. For 364 days a year, it served good wine but had a hard time selling more than five bottles a week. It was the early 1970s, and the customers hadn't quite made the connection between good food and a glass of wine to go with it. We did serve a lot of martinis and drinks with cherries in the bottom. We also sold a lot of bottled beer.

One day a year, as soon as possible after November 16, we gave a party to celebrate the release of the new Beaujolais. It was usually raw and sulphurous. It smelled unwholesome and left your mouth feeling like suede. It had a lot of character but all of it bad.

On that one day a year, we sold about 400 bottles of Nouveau. We sold it by the bottle, and people bought it and swigged it down like soda pop. There was music and dancing; it was one of the best parties in town. Folks who never drank wine were spattered with the stuff, and I suspect there was a lot of absenteeism from work the next day.

The Nouveau Beaujolais that made all this wretched excess possible was made that year from the Gamay grape and released to the public on November 16. It's not a wine that's had much time to develop much finesse; sometimes it was bottled while it was still fermenting. It didn't have any body, and in bad years, the flavor reminded you of paint thinner. The excitement it caused can best be attributed to harvest frenzy, coupled with some very shrewd promotion on the part of the growers.

Today's Nouveau is better made than the vintages of the 1970s. Sometimes it's delicious, but the quality is still highly variable. The parties, I'm glad to say, have also gotten better, and some chefs have even thought out the problem of making a menu to go with the new wine.

Nouveau doesn't really taste like other wines. There's something fresh and assertive about the flavors, and the bouquet is often strongly chemical. It's hard to imagine that this wine comes from a vineyard; you almost suspect a factory and a chemist or two involved. You wouldn't be surprised to hear that the same place that made the Nouveau also made toaster tarts and some kind of candy that glows in the dark.

Relax. There is some magic going on here, but it's perfectly benign. What happens is that grapes from the field are loaded into a tank and covered with an atmosphere of carbon dioxide. Under the blanket of gas, the grapes stay alive and begin to metabolize their own sugar into alcohol without the help of yeast. The grapes can produce as much as 2 percent alcohol all by themselves. While they're at it, they also produce byproducts like glycerol, methanol (wood alcohol), and acetylaldehyde, which can sometimes give the wine a paint-thinner aroma.

Meanwhile, down at the bottom of the tank, some of the grapes have been crushed by the weight of the ones above. Their juice comes in contact with the yeast on the skins, and a regular fermentation starts. After a week or so, the tank is emptied, and all the grapes are crushed and the juice collected. The juice that fermented inside the grape is mixed with the stuff that was already fermenting, and the whole tank ferments rapidly to completion. The process is called **carbonic maceration.** It preserves a lot of the freshness of the grapes and accounts for the cidery vigor of the wine. Its power to create a whole slew of flavor chemicals is why the Nouveau tastes so peculiar.

More important than its immediate flavor impact, it's a wine that can teach you something. When you pour your first glass out of the bottle, the chemical aromas are overwhelming: Some tasters spontaneously dip their napkins in it and start cleaning the mirrors. Then if somebody finds a pitcher and pours a whole bottle into it with a lot of splashing and purple bubbles, in a few minutes, a happy little fruit wine will plop its way into the glass.

Farmer in Beaujolais, France

Other regions with an abundance of lightly flavored grapes are following the lead. There's Novello from Italy and Junker (*yunker*) from Arnold Schwarzenegger's native Styria.

Beaujolais Village. Carbonic maceration and fresh fruit flavors are also characteristic of this more refined drink from the hilly central part of the Beaujolais district. The extra finesse comes from better vineyards, lower yields, and also from its not being pressed early and hurried through fermentation. If the wine is no more than a year or two old, you can usually count on a reliable, tasty drink at a bargain price.

Cru Beaujolais. Vastly underappreciated, these wines come from the best vineyards in the northcentral part of the region. They can show remarkable concentration and longevity while still boasting a bundle of Gamay flavor. At this writing, they are about twice as costly as a Nouveau Beaujolais and are, for the fruity-wine lover, a great bargain.

Unfortunately, they usually don't carry the name Beaujolais on the label. To find them, you will have to remember their individual names: Brouilly, Côtes de

Brouilly, Chenas, Chiroubles, Fleurie, Julienas, Moulin-à-Vent, Morgon, Regnié, and St. Amour.

> Medical students and others who have had their memory taxed in youth might remember these with a mnemonic—a memory device that pays tribute to Mnemosyne, the Greek goddess of memory. Here's a bad one: Because Certain Crus Contain Flavored Juice, Many Monasteries Reject them Soundly. Each capital letter is the initial of a cru. I'm sure you can do better.

Grenache

If your grandfather made wine in the basement, there's a good chance that his favorite grape was Grenache. It's a red grape from Aragon in Northern Spain that made its reputation in the southern Rhône Valley in France. It's a viticulturalist's dream that fruits abundantly and is perfectly naturalized in California. If left unpruned, it makes a lot of high-sugar fruit on the vine and a lot of money for its growers.

But a profitable grape isn't necessarily a delicious one; in the United States at least, Grenache has been a fine-wine flop. Americans loved it for its ability to make a lot of juice in hot conditions. Even in France and Spain, Grenache is mostly used as a blending grape to add fruit and alcohol to fine wines made from more noble varieties. It puts some fruit in Tempranillo to make red wines in Spain, and it's an important part of all the quality blends in the southern Rhône. It's rare to find a wine in which Grenache dominates, even though fully ripe fruit from a closely pruned vineyard can make delicious wine with a white-pepper spiciness and cherry fruit flavor.

Exceptions are to be found in Catalonia, now a part of Spain, where some 100 percent Grenache appears in the concentrated wines of Priorat. In Sardinia, where the grape and the wine is called Cannonau, it makes a substantial, sun-kissed table wine. It's also the basis of the splendid fortified Banyuls from French Catalonia and a few graceful table wines from Jumilla and Aragon in Spain. In Sardinia, it is also unblended and is known as Cannonau. Grenache tends to be low in pigment and tannin.

Malbec

For a grape you may have never heard of, Malbec really gets around. It's a big deal in southwestern France, where it's probably native. It grows in the Loire and Bordeaux regions of France, too, but these cooler climates tend to give Malbec a coarse flavor.

Recently, it has been producing ripe, concentrated, and deeply pigmented wines in Argentina's Mendoza Province. There it's grown on a high plateau just east of the Andes. In the rain shadow of these mountains, the land has scant rainfall but lots of available water from the runoff of snow melt. That enables wine growers to control the amount of water that gets to the vines and thereby regulate the development of the grapes. This control, coupled with warm days and cool nights, has enabled Malbec to flourish. Early frosts remain a problem, but the boldness of winemakers like Nicola Catena have pushed Malbec to the front of the red wine list.

Merlot

Wine has its fashions. Tastes, like hemlines, go up and down, revealing and concealing. A few years ago, we saw the first evidence that red wine could actually be good for you. This prompted a lot of white wine drinkers to give the darker stuff a try. The more recent discoveries of how a daily glass of red wine is good for the cardiovascular system have provided a motivation to keep at it.

The problem for the neophyte is that red wines have lots of flavors and aromas and things that go "boomp" in your mouth. Even a mediocre red wine has more stuff going on than American white wine drinkers are used to. Thus, the newcomers gravitated to red wines that were softer, smoother, and less ambitious than the big reds that old-time red wine fans admired. The buzzwords were "easy-drinking" and "approachable."

As it happens, Merlot is one of the best grapes for making a soft red wine. In Bordeaux, Merlot was the peasant winemaker's insurance against a bad crop. It ripened earlier than the dominant Cabernet Sauvignon so it would survive an early frost, and it could produce fruit when wet weather or bad drainage reduced the Cabernet's yield. Fortunately for the Bordelaise winemaker, Cabernet and Merlot blend beautifully, and most great Bordeaux wines are a blend of the two.

In America, however, Merlot sometimes stands alone. Its hardiness in the vineyard and its smoothness in the bottle have made it this country's most widely planted red wine grape. Some of that output is weakly flavored and watery textured—exactly the kind of wine that appeals to the person who drinks red wine for the sake of his or her health.

So does that mean that there's no Merlot that's meant for the real wine lover? On the contrary, there are some rich, interesting Merlots out there. Just don't expect them to be cheap.

Nebbiolo

Nebbiolo is one of the greatest of grape varieties and one of the most local. It's hard to think of a good example of a Nebbiolo-based wine that's grown anywhere but in northern Italy. The wines are deeply colored in their youth—black rubies. As they age, they shade to garnet and then to orange-brick or onion skin. Youthful bouquets of cherries and tar transmute into tobacco, licorice, truffles, and leather. The wines tend to be hard when they're young, maturing into a combination of power and elegance. Nebbiolo shows up first of all in the wines of Barolo and Barbaresco from Piedmont. You may also see Ghemme, Gattinara, and Carema on a label. In other parts, it's known as Spanna, Chiavenasca, or Picotener.

This is a late-ripening variety that had a string of successful vintages in the 1990s. Good examples of Barolo and Barbaresco are necessarily expensive, but wines labeled simply "Nebbiolo" or "Nebbiolo d'Alba" can provide a reasonably priced way to discover what all the shouting is about.

Petite Sirah

The Petite Sirah variety first showed up in California vineyards in the 1880s. According to recent DNA mapping, it is a cross based on the Syrah grape of the northern Rhône and an obscure variety called Peloursin. It was originally created by a nurseryman named Dr. Durif, who propagated grape clones for the wine industry. He was impressed with this particular cross because it resisted downy mildew, a fungus that had been causing widespread damage to European vineyards since before 1878.

He named the variety after himself, and in spite of being mildewproof, it never became popular in France and doesn't exist there today. In the moist climate of the south of France, the grapes were prone to rot. The name "Petite Sirah" was coined in California by the nursery that imported it, the implication being that it was somehow Syrah's little sister.

Petite Sirah became popular with winemakers in California because its inky color, intense, peppery flavor, and abundant tannins were ideal for adding some muscle to wines designed for the jug trade. It was also relatively prolific, yielding a lot of fruit without a dilution of its intense flavor. By the turn of the century, Petite Sirah rivaled the two most popular wine grapes, Zinfandel and Mourvèdre (then called Mataro in California), in volume and acreage.

Don't confuse Petite Sirah with its ancestor, Syrah/Shiraz. Syrah's huge flavor makes it unlikely that you would mistake it for anything petite. It is plummier in flavor and more vulnerable to both overcropping and bad harvest timing. You may often end up with a lame, watery Syrah/Shiraz, but you'll never have a Petit Sirah that's not robust.

It seems to me that decanting, or pouring the wine off into another container to aerate it, is mandatory if you want to enjoy the full flavor and impact of Petite Sirah. Serving temperature should be a cool 60 to 65 degrees Fahrenheit. Don't worry if you find some sediment in the wine or clinging to the bottle; this is a highly pigmented wine and the sedimenting of pigment is purely natural.

Pinot Noir

A bottle of California Pinot Noir

This is the native grape of Burgundy. For centuries, the word *burgundian* meant rich and luxurious, and the Pinot Noir wines of Burgundy (sometimes suitably but illegally blended and fortified with wines from the south of France) were a substantial part of that association. Pinot Noir is Burgundy's native grape. Ninety years after the establishment of Roman wineries in the region, local wine was being shipped back as a rival to Rome's best. In 79 C.E., Mt. Vesuvius erupted, destroying the Italian equivalent of the Napa Valley, and imported Burgundy began its rise.

By the time Benedictine monks at Citeaux established their first vineyard in 1112 at Vougeot, the wines had only a local market. The monks developed the notion of *cru,* or the different grades of harvest from walled-in vineyards called *clos.* They made, sharecropped, and taxed wine. Other churchmen followed suit, and churches, as well as universities and hospitals, grew rich from the wine trade.

In the years since that reputation was earned, Pinot-based wines have undergone a change. They used to be fermented for twenty days, extracting lots of flavor and depth and making a wine that needed age as part of its recipe. Today, six to twelve days is more common, and the lighter wines are ready to drink earlier.

So what are these wines like today? Their most dominant characteristic is a beautiful bouquet: fruity, floral, rich, and well, Burgundian. In the mouth, the younger wines tend to be light at best, unsubstantial at worst. Outside of France, excellent wine is being made in places where the cool climate lets the grapes mature slowly. The necessity of pruning to reduce the crop keeps the cost of good Pinot Noir high no matter where it is grown.

Small amounts of Pinot Noir are grown in Champagne, where it is vinified without skin contact to make a white sparkling wine, and in the Loire Valley. In the United States, all the excitement seems to center on Pinots from Oregon, Washington, and Pennsylvania.

Sangiovese

Sangiovese is the grape that makes Chianti, which is the wine that most people think of when they think of Italy. Never mind that Chianti has a dozen different faces and no one seems to be able to say for sure just what it should taste like. There is something essentially Italian about this grape and the traditional light-to-medium finish of Chianti.

But even this is deceiving. Sangiovese could be considered a family of grapes. There are major variations like Brunello di Montalcino (see page 69) and hundreds of clones that are being developed and researched now as part of the Chianti 2000 project. Wines range in style from the monumental Brunello di Montalcino to some baby-faced Sangiovese Romagnas. All will deliver a distinct acidity and a slightly bitter tannic snap. It's the tannins that make Sangiovese such a perfect match for the acidity of Italian food. You can usually taste cherries, and well-ripened examples will have a touch of plum. In the middle of the last century, Sangiovese's wines often came to this country with a certain peasant roughness inside the straw-wrapped bottle, but that style, along with the straw, has virtually disappeared.

This is Italy's most widely planted red grape, and it forms the basis of most of the wine of the central region. Recently, Cabernet Sauvignon was being blended to give more structure or to add another dimension of fruitiness.

Syrah

When wine lovers talk about things other than wine, they sometimes use wine as a metaphor, as a way to take some ineffable experience and "eff" about it anyway. You can't really blame them; when you're smack up against how difficult the world can be to figure out, wine is both a good example and an excellent consolation.

So when wine lovers want to discuss the difference between power and finesse, they look for winey examples. On the power side, the first wines that come to mind are the ones made from the Syrah grape. These are wines that burst their way into your mouth with enormous flavors and leave your senses exhausted. The most common flavors encountered are a distinct smokiness (you are sometimes reminded of a house that just burned down) and very ripe plums.

Some of the most famous Syrah-based wines are made in the northern Rhône Valley in France. The greatest of these are rare, expensive, special-occasion numbers like Hermitage and Côte Rotie. The northern Rhône also produces the more common but extremely variable Crozes-Hermitage.

More reliable Syrahs come from California and Australia. The Australians call the grape Shiraz. Down there, Shiraz is the backbone of their greatest wines. In the New World, the winemakers' struggle seems to involve getting some nuances of flavor into the thick, dark taste.

One of the easiest wine/food pairings in the world remains Syrah/Shiraz with smoked foods like hams, Texas-style barbecue, and classic split pea soup. With the greater availability of home smokers these days, expect an upsurge in popularity of this grape.

Zinfandel

In the beginning, Zinfandel was an intensely flavored red grape that was loved by two different kinds of wine drinkers. Most of Zin's production went anonymously to big, red jug wines—the kind that sustained generations of graduate students, starving artists, and young couples with mortgages. Zinfandel is the most widely grown red grape in California, so that's a lot of wine.

The little bit that was left over was made, mostly by small wineries, into inky, intense, fruit-laden wines that were often very high in alcohol and loved by a small group: Think of them as the original "Zinners." The big Zinfandels were pretty much ignored by serious wine lovers. Part of the prejudice came from the fact that Zinfandel was not a famous European grape. In fact, until recently, ampelographers didn't have a clue about its ancestry. Genetic testing has recently connected it to Primitivo, an obscure Italian variety, and both of them seem to be derived from a native Croatian grape called Crljenik Kasteljanski (kurlyenik kastelyansky). Both of these styles got their dark color from allowing the grape juice to sit on the crushed grapes and extract the red color.

A few years back, red jug wine gave way to the taste for white. All of a sudden, acres of Zinfandel grapes were going unloved, and worse yet, unused. Some of the orphaned surplus got diverted to making a white or a blush wine. These wines are easier to make than reds because the grape juice is pumped off the fruit right after the crush, not sitting around lounging on the skins, drawing out flavor and color. Most of this wine is slightly sweet and low in flavor: There's a lot of flavor along with the color in the grape skin. One of the weird consequences of this is that a whole generation of drinkers grew up thinking that Zinfandel was a white wine.

In the last fifteen years, dozens of wineries in California, led by Ridge and Ravenswood, have begun to make wines that take advantage of the Zin's potential. Zinfandel can be grown under a wide range of conditions, and practically the full spectrum of wine styles can be made from it.

The really good news for wine lovers is that a few winemakers have learned to get the best that this grape has to offer. Zinfandel at its best can be a hugely flavored, fruity and earthy wine with lots of spicy subtleties. It is not very expensive compared to other wines of the same quality, and it is ready to drink as soon as you buy it.

White-Wine Varieties

Chardonnay

At a wine tasting, I asked the nice young sommelier with the perfectly shaven head what he thought of Chardonnay. He pursed his lips and said, "I sell a lot of it, but I never drink it." He drew out the word "never" to make sure I understood.

At a charity dinner, I asked a beautiful brunette the same question. "Chardonnay?" she said. "It reminds me of my ex-sister-in-law." How's that? "Boring and a little bit sour."

I ask the man in the wine shop what his best selling variety is. "Chardonnay, hands down." So what's going on here? How can a grape that people snicker about provide the best selling varietal wine in the store?

Maybe it's because Chardonnay's flavors are easy to understand: toasty, creamy vanilla from those oak barrels, apple and pear, citrus and tropical fruits. Perhaps it has a taste that fits in at cocktail time. Or it could be that its charms are best suited for the occasional wine drinker—and that's what most people are. My snooty respondents just drink enough to get tired of the easy, greasy taste of a smooth white wine.

On the other hand, if you're looking for really overblown, weirdly flavored grape-based alcoholic beverages, go to the New World Chardonnay shelf. Rosés aside, there's more pukey excess here than anywhere. There are wines that taste like guava juice and vodka, and others that remind you of vanilla extract, caramel candy, butterscotch, and lemons.

These bizarre tastes are disconcerting for people who have been exposed to the original Chardonnay-based wines, the ones from Burgundy in France. Those wines are sometimes austere, sometimes refined, and sometimes disappointing, but they always taste like wine.

What's the source of all this weirdness? Part of it comes from the warmer weather in California. The heat produces a grape that develops more overblown flavors. Another source is the widespread American use of sulphur dioxide as an antioxidant when the juice is first extracted. The preservative keeps more of the "primary" grapy flavors alive and prevents the formation of the more "mature" winey tastes.

And then there's oak. People have been storing wine in oak for hundreds of years—it's a trick the Gauls taught the Romans. Originally, oak barrels were desirable simply because they weighed so much less than the pottery jars (amphorae) that they replaced and made it less expensive to transport wine. Eventually, the barrel came to be prized because it added its own flavor to the wine. The expensive barrels were used and reused until, like a used teabag, most of the flavor was soaked out of them and the effect on the wine was subtle. American winemakers use oak chips and new barrels from strongly flavored native oak, and the effect can be anything but subtle. Many modern wine drinkers end up not recognizing the difference between the taste of the barrel and the grape.

Since many people still like their wines on the easy drinking side, the wine industry has responded with a lot of cheap, good Chardonnay. Remember that the finest of these wines taste their best when they're a little warmer than refrigerator temperature. Avoid putting them in an ice-and-water-filled bucket; they'll end up so cold that the flavors won't come through.

Chenin Blanc

Chenin Blanc is a grape that has made a lot of cheap, drinkable white wine. It can play this role because even in the very hot climate of a place like the Central Valley in California, where vineyards are irrigated and yields per acre can be economically astronomical, Chenin Blanc keeps its cool; that is, it conserves its naturally high acidity. Without acid, white wines, especially high-sugar, warm-climate ones, can taste grossly flabby.

In Vouvray in the Loire Valley of France, where too much sunshine is rarely the problem, this high acidity is a blessing in the few years where the grapes achieve a creditable ripeness. It even makes possible an occasional dessert wine bargain like Côte de Layon. In the United States, some of the best Chenin Blancs come from Washington state, where a cool and more regular growing season allows the grape to show off its best at remarkably low prices.

Pinot Grigio/Pinot Gris

The Italian version of this poor little grape is widely known for its insipidity (from the Latin *insipidus,* meaning "you might as well drink vodka"). Wine-growers like it for its ability to ripen to high sugar levels in a short growing season and its ability to sustain high yields. The Rulander clone of the grape—a

German import—is doing wonderful things in Italy's Alto Adige, and while it may never reverse Pinot Grigio's reputation, it's worth seeking out.

In Alsace in the most northeasterly corner of France, it is known as Pinot Gris (gree). In this strip of land along the Rhine, it makes some very serious and very seriously undervalued elegant wines in styles that range from bone-dry to luxuriously sweet. The first interesting American attempts—lots of fruit and medium body—are based on the French clones of the grape, and some interesting stuff is turning up in Oregon's Willamette Valley. These new wines have a more concentrated fruity flavor and a bit of body.

Riesling

A bottle of German Riesling wine

Riesling is the star of the German winemaking show, an early-ripening cool-climate grape. In some especially cold places, it takes a longer time to mature, producing as it does a host of interestingly nuanced flavors. These most northerly wines are necessarily low in alcohol, but they have a tremendous potential for aging. They are also the wines that flop most dramatically in unfavorably cool years and therefore become even rarer and more expensive.

In Germany, levels of quality are determined by the degree of sweetness in the grape; that is, the riper the better. In the past, German winemakers showed off their sugar by retaining as much of it as possible in the wine and did so at the expense of the alcohol levels. More recently, there is a trend toward dry, dinner-friendly wines that are labeled *trocken,* but even these wines have a small dose (up to .9 percent) of sugar retained.

The dominant impressions of the best German Rieslings are crisp acidity and grape sugar. The bouquets are flowery, and there is often a mineral tang and a slightly oily texture and smell.

In Alsace, France's most German region, the winemaker's intent is to create power and alcohol and to drive out the overt prettiness that the Germans prize. This is accomplished by warm fermentations that go to completion.

In the United States, Riesling was used for years to produce a light-flavored, moderately sweet wine aimed at the beginning wine drinker. Recently, winemakers are emphasizing the grape's ability to produce a lot of sugar in the long California summer. The wines they make are often dessert wines. In the cooler-climate states—Oregon, Washington, and New York—there is a lot of experimentation centered on aromatic table wines.

Sauvignon Blanc

Sauvignon Blanc is a native of the Loire Valley of France. It is one of the most easily recognized varieties thanks to its sharp, distinctive bouquet. That bouquet can include grassy and vegetable notes that result from the presence of tiny amounts of a chemical called methoxypyrazine. Keep that odd smell in check and a whirl of citrus, tropical fruit, and even fig flavors emerge to hang on a structure that includes a lot of crisp acidity.

The key to keeping the grass out of your glass is in removing leaves that shade the fruit clusters after they appear and in finding shallow, relatively unfertile soils. Less water also makes for smaller (and fruitier) fruit.

The best French Sauvignon Blancs tend to be relatively austere, with the characteristic bouquet backed up by small amounts of fruit flavor. Really lush Sauvignons are being made today in New Zealand, particularly in the area around Marlbourough. These wines have made such an impact on the market that the style is being widely copied in Australia and California.

In the late 1970s, Robert Mondavi decided that Sauvignon was too hard for Americans, especially the men, to pronounce, so he rechristened his wine made from the variety as Fumé Blanc. Sales increased, and now other wineries use the new name, too. Wines with the new name are said to be more frequently oak-aged, but the real difference is in what is easier to pronounce in the restaurant or wine shop.

Another style of Sauvignon Blanc is emerging in eastern Europe, especially in Austria's Wachau Valley. Made from old, low-yielding vines it is deeply concentrated with a fruit and honey character that is laced with herbs and minerals.

It's both an earthy and a fruity style that probably owes a lot to terroir. We'll see soon how successfully it can be copied elsewhere.

Sauvignon is known to come into its own when fish is being served, especially if the preparations are simple and without sauce. What is less appreciated is its role as a cocktail wine before dinner. The very best of the Savignon Blancs have a bundle of interesting fruit tastes without the cloying sweetness that can kill an appetite. The least (and least expensive) will be cool, tart, and refreshing.

Discussion Questions

- The proof, of course, is in the tasting. Assemble examples of different varietals of the same color from the same winemaker. Organize a tasting and identify exactly what separates the Chardonnay from the Riesling or the Cabernet Sauvignon from the Zinfandel.

- Understand how genetic variations like bud sports lead to entirely new populations of grapes and how this affects the industry.

Glossary

barrique Oak barrel holding 24 cases, wine stored in barriques picks up flavor from the wood and also from the small amounts of air that infiltrate the barrel. Originally used in France, barriques nowadays are employed all around the winemaking world.

carbonic maceration A kind of fermentation in which crushed grapes begin to ferment inside their own skins. The result is a fresh, fruity wine that is drinkable immediately but doesn't age well.

clos A vineyard enclosed by a stone wall. Originally used in Burgundy, the term has been borrowed freely (and loosely) in the United States.

cru On a French wine label refers to a ranking, 1er cru means first rank., etc.

varietal A wine made mostly from a single grape variety. In the United States, a wine must contain 75% of the variety named on the label.

varieties Named, genetically distinct populations of grape vines: Barbera, Blaufrankisch, Brunello, etc.

Chapter 6

Winemaking

When you finish this chapter, you will:

- *Have a basic understanding of fermentation as the source of alcohol and esters in wine.*
- *Understand the centrality of good grapes in making good wine.*
- *Know the difference between making red wine and white wine.*
- *Know which choices the winemaker makes as grape juice turns into wine.*
- *Understand the complex roles that wooden barrels play in creating the flavor of modern wine.*
- *Know how acidity can be controlled in the winemaking process.*
- *Understand the roles played by filtering, fining, and stabilization before bottling.*
- *Be familiar with how champagne is made.*

Winemaking

A lot of people who work in wineries call themselves winemakers, but most of them use the term with a slight sense of irony. They know that the real winemakers are tiny, ubiquitous, single-celled organisms called yeasts. Since long before there were people who called themselves winemakers, even long before there were the creatures that we now call people, yeasts were busy making wine. Any ripe grape whose skin is broken leaks some juice, and that juice comes in contact with yeast that grows on the skin of the grape or with yeast cells in the air. The process of fermentation starts, and fermentation, as we know, makes wine. This is true no matter how the grape is crushed—by humans, animals, or hailstones. Wine is older than we are.

Ancient winemaking

So we don't really make wine. Grapes make wine, and yeast makes wine, and time makes wine, too. This doesn't mean that the winemaker has no role. She has, in fact, dozens of choices, and it's these choices that we're talking about when we discuss winemaking.

The basic life work of yeast is the process of devouring sugars, excreting alcohol and carbon dioxide, generating heat, and reproducing more yeast cells. In a sugary solution, yeast will continue this useful work until the sugar is all used up or the alcohol content of the solution reaches a point where it renders the yeast inactive. For most wild yeasts, that point is at 4 or 5 percent alcohol. A properly bred wine yeast, on the other hand, will continue its useful labor until an alcohol level of at least 12 percent is reached (or all the sugar in the juice is consumed).

There is a certain miraculous utility about yeast that makes it worthy of at least a moment's contemplation. The tiny size of yeast cells and their ability to dry out without dying help to make them ubiquitous. They float in the air and inhabit the surface of everything. Because of this happy property, it took no particular genius on our part to make use of yeast's blessings. It intruded itself upon us. Be thankful.

Airborne yeasts probably made the first breads. They certainly made the first ales and wines. Because of their one-celled simplicity, yeasts could be easily harvested from liquid products like wine and beer, dried, and revivified for later use. They can also be selectively bred like cattle, carnations, or Kerry Blue Terriers. So we have champagne yeasts and sherry yeasts, ale yeasts, and lager yeasts. Yeast is bred for its tolerance to alcohol, for ability to thrive in a particular range of temperatures, or for the flavor it contributes to the final product. Recent developments include a quick-acting yeast that cuts most bread rising times in half and a special champagne yeast that may eventually reduce the cost of champagne a little. Again, be thankful.

Remember, yeast eats sugar and gives off alcohol and carbon dioxide (CO_2). In bread making, the alcohol formed is evaporated in baking; in winemaking, the CO_2 is released into the air, and in beer making, both products are preserved. This is, like most group biographies, a simplified version. In reality, there are vitamins, enzymes, nutrients, and intermediate steps involved. Yeast does different things in the presence of oxygen than it does in its absence. There is also more than one kind of sugar and several varieties of alcohol. There are even some sugars that are nonfermentable.

The Vineyard

The choices begin in the vineyard with the selection of a grape variety to plant. The variety has to be one that thrives in the climate of that particular vineyard and in the structure of that vineyard's soil. Soil structure is more important to vines than soil chemistry, although there are seventeen distinct nutrients that wine grapes require. Vines need soil that is well-drained and deep. That kind of soil, gravel or broken limestone, forces the root to grow deep in the ground and prevents the vine from being overwatered and producing too many leaves and water-stuffed fruit.

Vineyard keepers also strive to keep the vines from being too leafy. Leaves inside a vine's canopy don't get enough light to support their own needs, so rather than contribute to the overall health of the crop, they actually subtract energy from the vine. Dense (unpruned) vine canopies also cause shading of the grapes, which leads to decreases in sugar, tartaric acid, and flavor-producing phenols. Shade also increases the amount of malic acid, raises the pH, and contributes to a grassy character in the wine. When you visit a vineyard making high-quality wine, expect to see a leaf canopy that you can see through.

Vines work hard in the summer. The leaves are busy turning sunshine into the sugar that will eventually ferment and become alcohol. The roots, meanwhile, are creating the flavors that make wines taste different from each other and different from any old alcohol-fortified beverage.

What makes winemakers nuts is that these two processes don't always work in tandem. Sometimes a hot, sunny summer will have the grapes at their maximum sugar level too early, before the flavor has a chance to develop further. This is a problem that California wineries sometimes have to deal with. The

Chambourcin vineyard—Chaddsford Winery

reverse situation is when the flavors are ripe but the year hasn't given enough sunshine to make enough alcohol to support them and preserve the wine. French winemakers in Bordeaux know all about that one: Their laws allow them to add sugar to the unfermented wine to make up the lack.

The year 1997 in California looked like one of those too-much-sun-too-early years. Potential alcohol levels were through the roof while the grapes were still underflavored. There were predictions of boozy, insipid wines—the kind of harvest that hurts the top-quality producers the most.

Then the rains came. Sugar levels stopped dead in their tracks. Harvests were delayed for two weeks and more, and a huge sigh of relief rose on the land. The rain was a mixed blessing. Some growers in low-lying valley areas with poor drainage lost their crops to rot. Many growers lost some grapes to rot and just pruned the bad ones away and harvested the rest.

> "After about 24 percent sugar, we stop paying attention to the numbers and start tasting for flavors and aromas."
>
> —Peter Luthy, Winemaker, Trefethen Vineyards

The unique timing of the weather produced a huge crop of high-quality grapes. Some of the biggest beneficiaries were growers of Zinfandel. Zin makes great wines from a wide range of ripenesses, and the 1997 Zins tended to be what the label writers call "opulent"—rich, thickly textured, and impressive with lots of ripe, plummy fruit. It was a year in which wineries that usually make a good, dependable product ended up with a great, or at least dramatic, one.

Another choice involves yield manangement, the slippery math that pits the quantity of grapes grown against their quality (see The Cost of Wine on page 117.)

Picking

Grape boxes

High-quality winemaking requires cool, ripe, unbruised fruit. Determining ripeness remains an area where science must be used artfully. Along with tasting to determine flavor and a visual examination for color, the viticulturalist may use an index like the ratio of acid to sugar to determine picking time. Examining grape seeds—called *pips*—is another tool. Unripe grapes have green pips. You can even chew the pips and taste the unripeness as a harsh, bitter flavor.

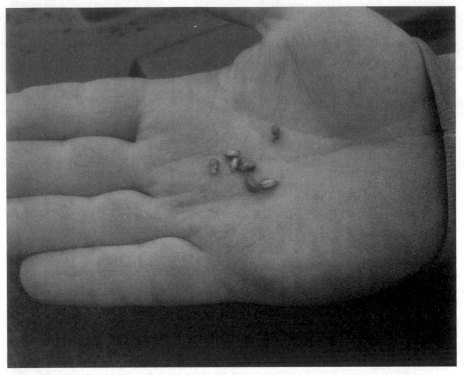

Unripe pips

The most careful vineyards pick in the early morning hours and use hand-picking or employ expensive harvesters that handle the grapes without breaking them. Industrial winemaking operations can cut costs by using giant harvesters that pick and crush the grapes in a single operation, delivering juice to the winery, instead of grapes.

> "The most important part of picking is handling the fruit gently."
> —Doug Shafer, Shafer Winery

The Winery

Crushing

Most of the time, grapes are mechanically crushed to get the juice in contact with the yeast. (See the section on Gamay on page 70 for an exception.) The old-fashioned way was to crush the grapes by stomping on them, a very slippery business. Notice the strap-hanging in the illustration at the head of this chapter. Bunches of grapes can be destemmed before crushing, or the stems can be left on to impart extra tannin to the wine. If the bunches are stripped of their stems, a measured weight of stems may be added later to the fermenting juice. The juice of the crushed grapes is called the **must**, and we are now on our way to making wine.

There are several options available for handling the must. Red wine gets its color, a protective dose of tannin, and a lot of its flavor from the red skins of the grapes, so the crushed grapes for, let's say, a Pinot Noir will be left in the must to extract as much flavor and color as possible. If the harvest has been overproductive and the must is too dilute, some of the juice may be removed (bled off) to concentrate the effect of skin contact with the rest.

Fermentation

Fermentation may be allowed to proceed naturally: In most Italian and French wineries, the juice contacts the yeast on the skin of the crushed grapes and nature does the rest. But a winemaker may be unhappy with his local yeast, and in

Fermenting cab with chips

the Americas and Australia, it's more common to kill off the local favorites with a dose of potassium metabisulfate and inoculate the wine with a specially cultured yeast.

Red wines will be allowed to ferment on their skins, and sometimes oak chips are added to the fermenting must. If a white wine is being made, the juice is pressed out of the solids and conveyed to a fermenter, which was traditionally made of wood. These days, a double-walled tank of stainless steel with refrigerant circulating between the walls is more common. The cooling absorbs the heat given off by fermentation and helps preserve fresh fruity flavors, especially in white wines.

This is the time when wines that are deficient in natural sugar get a boost. Sugar can be added: 20 grams per liter increases alcohol levels by 1 percent. This process, known as *chaptalization* for J-A Chaptal, the Napoleonic official who authorized its use in France in 1801, smacks of artificiality and gives New World winemakers, who rarely practice it, a chance to sniff at European winemakers, who do. All posturing aside, chaptalization can improve the balance of an otherwise excellent wine.

Chaptalizing

Germany and Australia do not permit the use of sugar, but they do allow for the addition of concentrated grape juice, or *süssreserve*. This sounds better than chaptalization, but for red wines at least, it dilutes color and flavor.

It's also possible to take a page from generations of North American cider makers and partially freeze the unfermented must. The part that freezes first will be lower in sugar and can be removed, concentrating the remainder. This isn't a great technique for red wines, but it works well for whites.

Finally, it is possible to remove some water from the juice by reverse osmosis, but nobody is bragging about doing so just yet.

Maceration

After fermentation is complete, new red wine may be left in contact with the skins and stems to extract more tannin and color. Winemakers now boast of extended maceration times on their websites: I saw a claim of 45 days not long ago. White wines are rarely macerated, but they may be allowed to remain in contact with the population of yeasts (the *lees*), which adds complexity to the flavor and prevents development of off-odors.

Pressing

Sooner or later, red-wine must is extracted from the solids, which are now called *pomace*. The "first-run" juice that was released by crushing is considered the best. Wine that's extracted by pressing or centrifuging is going to be more tannic. Some great red wines are made entirely from first-run juice; others have judicious amounts of press wine added so the tannins can protect them.

The pomace can be reused. A small amount of sugar can be extracted by washing the pomace with water. This lightly sweet liquid can then be fermented and distilled. Grappa (in Italy) and Marc (in France) are made this way.

Maturing

If you listen to wine geeks long enough, you'll eventually hear the words "wood" and "oak" used to describe the taste of wine. For most normal people, this a very strange use of language—the kind of talk you might expect to hear from beavers and termites. But wine gets to taste a little like wood because some wines are stored and matured in oak barrels. Some of the flavor of wood leaches into the wine. But wait, there's more. Barrels are charred before the wine goes in, and the fire gives a toasty caramel flavor to the wood just like heat toasts a piece of bread. Wooden barrels are porous, too, and a little bit of wine evaporates through the staves and a little bit of air gets in. This controlled oxidation also adds flavor, making the grapy fruit tastes more complex and subtle. We're still not done: In a dry climate, the water fraction of the wine evaporates more rapidly than the alcohol, so barrel aging can actually raise the concentration of alcohol. In damp climates—cool caves, for instance—some alcohol can actually be lost. Both of these evaporation effects can be used to affect the taste of the wine.

What does it mean to say that a wine tastes like oak? Most wine lovers build up a sense of what that silly-sounding expression might mean by tasting a lot of wine and trying to parse out the common factor in the wines that everyone else calls woody. After a few hundred wines, you get a feel for it, but you really can't be sure.

The nice folks at Robert Mondavi have taken some of their Chardonnay and aged it for one year in six different batches. These batches aren't sold in stores, but they're made available to groups for tastings. The first, in stainless steel, has a light, musky bouquet with hints of fruit. Then it hits your mouth like a big, sour, acid bomb that gives way to a grapy flavor. The second, in a French oak barrel that had been used for eight years, rounded over all these hard tastes. It is still acidic, but the flavors seem more integrated. The wine is more subtle and a lot more fun to drink. The third batch, in new American oak, smells like something between a fireplace and an ashtray. The flavor reminds me of chewing on a toothpick. The fourth wine, in heavily toasted French oak, has a bouquet of vanilla and butterscotch and a mineral-caramel set to the flavor—a very pleasant wine. The fifth and sixth wines are from medium-toasted barrels, one French, one American. The French barrel gives a light citrus flavor, and the American has a touch of vanilla.

So what do we learn from this tasting? It's pretty clear that dry Chardonnay by itself is an unlovely customer: sour and simple. Any aging diminishes the intensity of the acid. Aging in old oak barrels rounds and integrates the existing flavors. New barrels give a forward fireplace aroma and taste. Wine from toasted barrels tastes more like vanilla or butterscotch and less like raw wood.

Is there wood in your wine? Most American Chardonnays in the $10 and up range have a healthy dose. See if you can taste it. In red wines, the effect of wood aging is more likely to show up as a silky vanilla character, and wood usually plays a smaller role in the taste of red wines.

Sometimes smaller is bigger: The smaller the barrel, the greater the ratio of wood surface to the volume of wine and the more pronounced the effect of wood. Newer barrels and ones made from American oak also make for more woodiness.

The Other Fermentation

The new wine has a pretty heavy dose of acid. Tartaric acid predominates, followed by malic acid, which is also found in apples. A malic acid molecule has two hydrogen radicals, each of which makes a donation to the overall acid impression of a wine. There is a second fermentation, a bacterial one called the *malolactic,* which turns malic acid into lactic acid. The latter has only one hydrogen to contribute and so is half as sour. Malolactic fermentation also contributes a butterscotch flavor to the wine.

Tartaric acid is rare in nature, so when archaeological chemists like Patrick McGovern find it on a shard of pottery from Godin Tepe in the Zagros Mountains of Iran, they can be pretty sure that the original vessel contained wine.

Almost all red wine undergoes the "malo" naturally. A few warm-weather whites may be discouraged from it to preserve their crispness. In emergencies, it can be induced by an introduction of bacteria and a raise of temperature.

Blending

Wines from different barrels, barrels from different vineyards, and vineyards with different varieties can all contribute to the composition of a wine. The elusive "balance" that we discussed in Chapter 2 is often achieved here by blending different lots of wine.

Some of the potential goals of blending are:

- To raise or lower alcohol levels. For years, truckloads of heavy, high-alcohol wine from the south of France and Algeria found their way to Burgundy to boost weak alcohol levels and improve color.
- To improve the color of the wine. Varieties like Petit Verdot in France and Colobel in North America are grown just for this purpose.
- To add or minimize flavors and tastes. Blends from the southern Rhône Valley in France are often constructed from several varieties, each of which may contribute only a single noticeable character to the wine.
- To adjust the pH of a wine. Low pH is necessary for wines to resist bacteria and oxidation. This is particularly important during fermentation.
- To lower or raise acidity. Acidity isn't the same as pH. Tests for total acidity measure both the free and bound hydrogen in a must.
- To balance the barrel-aged character of a wine. A little new oak goes a long way, so winemakers frequently blend batches from older and younger barrels to achieve a more complex character.
- To adjust tannin levels and tannin character. This is sometimes just a matter of blending a wine with too much tannin for its fruit with one that has less tannin.

"When you blend, you have to be willing to abandon some of your wine. Some vintages are extremely difficult that way."
—Chris Howell, Winemaker, Cain Vineyards

Filtering, Fining, and Stabilization

We could blame it on the Victorians, I guess, but we seem to have a passion for limpid liquid. In recent years, we have seen clear gasoline, clear soaps, clear mouthwashes, and clear soft drinks. All of these products are marketed without the slightest suggestion that clarity affects the taste or performance of the products themselves. Maybe it's nothing more than evidence of fashion's insatiable appetite for the new. (It's New! It's Clear!) Perhaps it's an indication of a longer cycle change, one that takes us further from the natural roots of things and deeper into a celebration of our own manufacturing.

This has created a market in which cautious wine merchants prefer to sell only wines that are crystal clear, so cautious winemakers oblige them by filtering the wine to remove the slightest haze. To be fair, filtering also removes bacteria that can threaten the wine in the bottle. Filtering involves moving the wine through a fine paper pad that can remove particles as small as one micron, a thousandth of a millimeter.

Fining is, in a way, the reverse of filtering. The wine stays in place, and an agent like beaten egg whites, isinglass, or powdered clay is sprinkled on top and the finings pass through the wine. As they sink, they carry impurities with them to the bottom of the tank, and the wine is siphoned off.

Cold stabilization involves chilling the wine and deliberately creating the tartarate crystals that can scare the uninitiated. These are then filtered out.

> If you ever have the chance to taste a filtered and unfiltered version of the same wine, jump at it. The evident brightness and complexity of the unfiltered wine will give you pause, or at least cause for pause. In any case, I worry that all these clear products may lead to cloudy judgment, and we may begin to confuse one with the other. Maintain vigilance; keep your clears straight—don't rinse after meals with the gasoline or mix rum and a slice of lime with detergent. And drink unfiltered wine when you can.

Making Champagne

In 1668, the Benedictine abbey of Hautvilliers was struggling to recover from the Thirty Years' War. The abbey had subsisted for years by housing and feeding pilgrims who visited the abbey's holy relic. The growth of Protestantism had eroded the pilgrim business. The abbey was struggling to sell its wine to Paris, England, and Flanders in competition with Burgundy. Their white wine, made from the red grape Pinot Noir, was better than the red from the same grape, so the monks tried to make the whitest wine possible from their red grapes. They developed some specialized techniques to do this:

Bottle of Moet & Chandon champagne

- Direct pressing—no maceration. It was necessary to have a fast, efficient press, which was a major capital investment. The monks could afford this kind of machinery, but the cost was too much for the individual grape-growing peasants.
- Blending for consistency. Because the abbey owned many vineyards and could buy grapes from many more, they were able to blend different wines together to achieve a consistent taste.
- No maturation in new wood. Time in wood destroys the delicacy of these wines so they had to be bottled in the fall or casked in old barrels for bottling in the spring.

This last point was at the heart of the invention of champagne as we know it. In the fall after harvest, the wine sometimes contained some unfermented sugar, particularly if fermentation was halted by an early cold snap. When spring came, the warmth would reactivate the yeast, and fermentation would restart. There was no place for the carbon dioxide to escape to and so pressure built up. If bottled, the corks popped or bottles exploded.

A stronger bottle was a partial answer. High-temperature glassmaking, developed by the English mystic Kenelm Digby, resulted in a bottle that could contain the pressure. There remained the problem of those bubbles. French taste at first decried them: The beauty of the wine was, for them, in its brightness and aroma. But in England, the popular taste embraced the fizz, and all further developments in champagne making are devoted to preserving champagne's bubbles.

The modern method of champagne production began in the early nineteenth century. In the champagne method, a light-bodied wine is made from high-acid grapes and then bottled with a small additional dose of sugar syrup added. This syrup ferments and produces a small amount of carbon dioxide, which is trapped in the wine. The carbon dioxide in turn, produces small amounts of an ester called ethyl pyrocarbonate.

The wine is kept in cool cellars, where the bottles are inverted in racks and turned a fraction of a turn and shaken every day. This process, called *remuage*, causes the yeast and grape sediment to fall to the neck of the bottle. After an aging period of up to four years, the spent yeast is then removed from each bottle, another sweetening dose of sugar added, and the bottles recapped with sturdy wire-tied corks. All of these operations and delays make champagne expensive, and it should not be surprising that people have developed cheaper methods for making a sparkling wine.

In the *charmat* method, the second fermentation occurs in a large tank. The wine and its gas are then pumped under pressure into another tank, where it is clarified by refrigeration and filtered before bottling. It is also possible to introduce carbon dioxide from a cylinder to a tank of chilled wine and to bottle the result—which is how soft drinks are made.

Discussion Questions

- "Ripeness" in wine grapes is a bit more complicated than that same quality in any other fruit. Discuss the differences.
- Could you make a sparkling wine from apple juice? From table grapes?
- What does diamond-like clarity tell you about a wine? What doesn't it tell you?
- If a particular wine is very popular, and therefore very profitable, why don't other winemakers just make a duplicate of it?
- What are the five effects that barrel aging can have on wine?
- If you wanted to add the taste of barrel aging to your wine, why not just throw some oak chips in it and let it sit for a while?

Glossary

must—Newly crushed wine grapes or their unfermented juice.

Chapter 7

Rights, Wrongs, and Rituals

When you finish this chapter, you will:

- *Understand the importance of rituals in everyday life.*
- *Know what to expect and what to do when ordering wine in a restaurant.*
- *Appreciate the importance of storing wine properly.*
- *Know what the right serving temperature is for various kinds of wine.*
- *Know which glasses add to the pleasure of a wine and which don't.*
- *Understand what aging does to wine.*
- *Appreciate how the context in which wine is served affects its taste.*
- *Be prepared to buy and use the right kind of corkscrew.*

Next time you're in a restaurant, watch a server open and pour a bottle of wine. If he or she is at all experienced, you may notice something theatrical, almost balletic, about the performance. If you watch it a few times, you learn what to expect: There is a regularity, almost a **ritual**, for the service of wine in a public place. The form does not arise, as some people think, from a desire to mystify and intimidate. It exists because rituals have a remarkable utility.

Why do we have rituals? The purpose of a ritual is to transform our emotional and mental states in a particular direction. Rituals do this by manipulating either our behavior or our perception. We have calming, reassuring rituals and arousing, exciting rituals. Reassuring rituals, such as confessions and funerals, tell us that things are not so bad after all. Arousing rituals, such as the pregame show, the pep rally, and sexual foreplay, crank up our anticipation of some intense experience and add to our pleasure in it.

Wine rituals are supposed to be both arousing and reassuring. They start with the waiter's bringing the wine list and offering it, along with the menus. This forces someone into the role of host at the table.

Being handed the wine list puts many otherwise poised people into a mild panic. The responsibility! The potential embarrassment! The stage fright! Relax. You can handle this part of the ritual by remembering three rules.

The first is that you should not make yourself crazy worrying about food and wine matchups. (For more on pairing food and wine, see Chapter 8.) If there are more than two people at the table or if food orders are very diverse, it's unlikely that you'll please everyone. Go for the best bottle in your price range.

The second rule is don't ask the waiter. Even though it's tempting to consult with an expert, the waiter may not be at all knowledgeable and is not exactly disinterested. On the other hand, if the restaurant has a wine steward or sommelier (so-mel-YAY), you can assume that she has a professional level of knowledge.

The third rule is for those rare occasions where you are someone's guest at dinner and this person has deferred to you because of the reputation for superior wine knowledge that you gained from reading this book. You may not want to ask "How much are you willing to spring for?" and your host may not give you a budget. By all means, try to hand the list back to the host, perhaps making a few suggestions at different price points. If you can't wiggle out, it's usually safe to order something that costs two to three times the price of an average **entrée**.

If the pronunciation of the name is a problem, don't worry. You can either point to your selection or ask for it by its number on the wine list. Many restaurants, recognizing that neither you nor the server may be comfortable with the pronunciation of, let's say "Ciachetti Montepulciano 'Ghiacciaio'" put "bin" numbers in front of each wine name. The waiter brings the selected wine and shows the label to the host, who nods his assent if it is, in fact, the bottle he has chosen. The waiter opens the bottle, being careful to remove the metal **capsule** from the neck and to wipe away any corrosion or mold that has formed under the capsule. He presents the cork to the host, who may wish to check to see that it is moist and uncrumbled and has done its job of protecting the wine. If you're of a paranoid frame, you might want to check the printing on the cork to make sure that the name printed there confirms that the fabulously expensive bottle you ordered is actually the one you got. It's easy to switch labels, harder to counterfeit and change corks.

Since hardly anyone knows the real reason for the cork presentation, it seems ridiculously arcane, almost an invitation to parody. The actor Peter Sellers put the cork to his ear (maybe he heard the ocean). I know a wine critic who, when his sense of the ridiculous is sufficiently provoked, puts the cork in his mouth and chews it for a minute before pronouncing it excellent.

Showing the label

Cutting the capsule

Pulling the cork

Wiping the neck

Sampling the wine

The waiter then pours a one- or two-ounce portion for the host. In pouring, he will hold the bottle at its bottom-most and give it a slight twist at the end of the pour as he raises the neck of the bottle and keeps any wine drops from escaping onto the tablecloth. The host tastes it and approves. Then everyone else is served before the host's glass is filled.

> The most fashionable waiters today will hold the bottle with their thumb in the indentation at the bottom. This little hollow, called the "punt," is a relic of the days when bottles were blown from blobs of molten glass at the end of tubes. Their arched shape gave some extra strength to the bottle bottom and is retained today purely out of love of tradition. The fact that the punt also makes any given bottle look bigger is probably incidental.

If there is something wrong with the wine, the host mentions this to the waiter, who should provide another bottle. This return privilege is one to be exercised only when the wine is defective. You should not expect to be able to return a wine just because you discover that you don't like it.

The waiter will serve three to four ounces at a time for a red wine. He'll serve less for a white to prevent the portion from warming up in the glass. In no case will he fill the glass more than halfway.

You may notice that while all this pouring and presenting and tasting is going on, conversation at the table comes to a halt. All eyes are on the bottle and the taster. You may even see a discreet moistening of lips. If the wine is an appetizer, then the presentation ritual is the appetizer's appetizer. Amen.

Getting the Most from Your Wine

There are a few things that you need to know in order to increase your enjoyment of the wine you drink at home. You should consider proper storage, serving temperature, getting some air in the wine, the role of aging, and the best glasses.

Storage. The taste of wine is fragile. Heat, light, and too much air are the enemies. To keep them at bay, wine should be stored in a cool damp place. The dampness keeps the cork from drying out. Fortunately, ideal serving temperatures (see below) and storage temperatures are about the same.

You need to know that even the best wine in the world will taste dead and baked if it has been subjected to heat for as little as a day. Potential danger zones are the trunk of your car, an unchilled liquor store, the container on ship or truck, or a warehouse.

Try to buy your wine from a deeply air-conditioned store. If the staff is wearing sweaters in summer, that's a good sign. A separate chilled storage area is good, too. Of course, a chilly store is no guarantee that the wine was protected on every stage of its trip from the winery. It's good practice to ask the wine merchant how the wine is protected before he or she buys it.

Air. When wine is poured, it changes as it is exposed to the oxygen in the air. Specifically, the sharp tastes of acids and tannins that protected the wine in the bottle are oxidized and make way for the fruity tastes of the grape and for the other flavors that have developed. Just the fact that some air has dissolved in the wine also improves the flavor. (In fact, any noncarbonated drink tastes better if it's lightly aerated.) These two processes combine to give meaning to the silly-sounding phrase "letting it breathe."

Sometimes, a bottle of wine is opened and poured (**decanted**) into another vessel. The air incorporated in the wine by splashing it around is the agent of change. There is some controversy surrounding this practice. Almost everyone will allow that there is something wonderfully attractive about a faceted glass decanter glowing jewel-like at the side of a festive table. Not everyone agrees that decanting also improves the flavor of the wine. Some people maintain that the practice is ineffective and changes nothing about the wine. Others find it effective but deleterious and maintain that the subtlest flavors and aromas are burned off during this forced oxidation.

My experience has been that most wines are improved by decanting them; that is, by pouring them from their original bottle into another container with a lot of splashing and bubbling. You can buy a funnel whose bottom spout has a dozen small holes through which the wine squirts as you pour from the bottle to a decanter, aerating itself in the process. Failing that, simply swirling the wine around in the glass for a minute or two will improve the flavor.

> Try this experiment: Pour any noncarbonated beverage into a glass and allow it to stand overnight. The next day, taste it. Then pour the drink into another glass and then back again to its original glass. Taste again. Is there a difference? Does the freshly aerated drink taste better?

Remember, swirling has the additional advantage of jump-starting the bouquet. The wines of Spain's Priorat district, for instance, tan the flesh of your mouth when they're first opened. (I mean this almost literally. The same tannin that occurs in wine is used in a process called "tanning" to preserve animal skins.) A few hours in the air and they develop a wonderful richness and subtlety that justify their reputation. I have even been pleasantly surprised by a bottle of one of these wines that was opened one night and finished the next.

Not every wine will benefit from taking the airs, and those that do are only improved up to a point. Too much time in the air will turn dry wines sour.

Try decanting—pouring the wine into a second vessel before pouring it into glasses—to improve the taste of wines that seem too astringent or sour when first tasted. A wine may also be decanted if it has some sediment. The wine is decanted with a light behind it so the server can stop pouring when the sediment rises to the neck of the bottle. In a restaurant, this little piece of ritual can add to the fun of ordering wine. See the advice on aging below.

The same exposure to air that helps a wine open up also accelerates its decline. An opened bottle of red wine may last a day, but it will rarely last two days or more. If you would like to keep a bottle opened and drink, let's say, a glass a day, you can extend its open shelf life by pumping some of the air out of the bottle. There are a number of devices to help you do this. They all consist of a special rubber plug that goes in the bottle and a pump that forces the plug open when it is placed on top. The user pumps the air out and then removes the pump, which seals the plug. Bottles of wine closed this way can keep for a week, and this simple device enables you to have more than one wine with your dinner at home without having to discard spoiled wine or drink more than you want to.

There is also the delicate matter of deciding just what constitutes an improvement. In America, we tend to favor a certain smoothness and a silky mouth feel; we also tend to prefer a wine that strongly resembles the fruit from which it was made. Other people like harder edged or more subtly aromatic wines and think that the best thing to do with a good fruity wine is to spread it on bread.

The best way to deal with these differences is to experiment and form your own impressions. Everyone agrees that it's a good idea to pour off the wine and leave behind any sediment or wine-logged cork that may have sunk to the bottom of the bottle.

Age. Wine also changes slowly in the bottle. The change may be an improvement in flavor or a deterioration. The most dramatic changes are analogous to those produced by air; the edges get rounded over, and new, more complex tastes emerge. This, as opposed to mere hoarding, is the reason people have wine cellars. Sometimes you have to taste a wine when it's young, guess what it will taste like in a while, buy a bunch of it, and hope you guessed right.

For most wines, the changes are not improvements. Almost all of the world's wines are made to be consumed within a year or two. For a very few, special wines, the change may be an increase in complexity as new flavors develop in harmony with each other and the structure of the wine.

Usually an experienced taster can tell which wines will age well and which ones won't. Wines with a soft, fruity taste are best consumed young and will merely fade if stored for long. Candidates for aging are usually red wines with a lot of tannin and significant acid. It's easy to detect tannin, which comes mostly from the stems of the grapes. Tannin, which acts as a preservative, gives the wine astringency, the same mouth-puckering feeling you get from a cup of strong plain tea. Acid reveals itself by a distinct sourness. Of course, a wine that is all astringency and sourness would be best put down the drain, not down in the cellar. An ageable wine should be balanced by a good, fruity basic taste.

Context. Wine changes taste depending on what else you're tasting at the time. Sometimes you can use a flavor to enhance a wine's strengths; other times, you can use a food to disguise a weakness. Also, the very fact of having something else in your mouth changes your experience of taste. Roast meats, for example, make us less sensitive to sweetness and acidity and more sensitive to salt and bitter tastes. Cheese interferes with the action of tannin in the mouth and heightens the awareness of sweetness. Salty foods and sweet wines with an acidic bite are great together. Some flavors, like those of chocolate, artichokes, and asparagus, just ruin the taste of wine, and others, like hot peppers and soy sauce, present distinct challenges.

Historically, wine has been judged in the context of a cacophony of tastes. People ate when they drank and vice versa. Today, we're as likely to cleanse our palates, draw the blinds, and turn down the stereo when we taste. In fact, we have an event called a tasting, as if tasting weren't something we did all the time. You might have more fun if you tried food with your wine. Away from the dinner table, you might try fresh fruit, dried fruit, cheese, or bread.

Temperature. Everybody knows that you should serve red wines at room temperature and white wines from an ice bucket, and everybody's wrong. American rooms tend to be around 70°F in the winter and slightly warmer in the summer. Any red wine served at those temperatures is going to taste sour and over-alcoholic. Sensations of sweetness are also exaggerated, and subtleties in the bouquet are lost. If a wine has any faults, they're exaggerated by warm temperatures. This isn't a call to ice the claret. Cold temperatures accentuate bitterness and astringency so the tannin in red wine gets too much emphasis. In general, it's better to serve most red wines on the cool side, but not cold—around 60°F. More tannic reds should be served a few degrees warmer.

In white wines, it's hard to detect any aroma at 45°F or below, and at 40°F (refrigerator temperature), taste buds are anaesthetized by the cold. In the mid-50s, they lose their refreshing character, and their dominant acids get out of hand. Sparkling wines (see Chapter 4) are at their best between 45 and 55°F. So our customary service of red wine at room temperature and white at refrigerator temperature or colder has nothing to recommend it except convenience. In fact, the temperature of a cool, damp cellar is just right for most wines, with an additional slight chill taking care of the rest. This is unfortunate because very few of us have musty, chilly cellars at our disposal, and the appliance store does not sell a Slight Chill Box. (Although you can buy purpose-built wine storage cabinets called "caves.") Pity.

A strategy for the cellarless wine lover is to store any wine that you might want to serve in the immediate future in the refrigerator. Remove the bottle of red a half hour before opening, the white 15 minutes. You can speed things up without hurting the wine by placing the bottle in a water bath at the desired temperature. If these contrivances seem to rob things of their spontaneity, decant the wine into a pitcher and pour it into glasses. All that splashing takes the chill off and the wine warms up even more in the glass. If your patience really fails, it does so even more quickly in the mouth.

Some wineries are implanting a temperature-sensitive patch on their labels that tells the consumer when the wine inside is at the optimum temperature.

Glasses. A great deal of your experience of wine comes from the aromas that develop in the air above the surface of the wine. A glass that forces the wine to have a large surface area for its volume and then narrows to concentrate the vapors will increase the flavor experience. Glasses with a thin lip seem to interfere less with the taste of wine than thicker (and cheaper) glasses.

The shape of the glass makes a difference, too. Since we can only smell molecules that are in the air, the best wine-tasting glass is going to promote evapo-

Three types of wineglasses

ration by exposing the largest possible surface area to the air. These glasses are wide at the waist and narrow at the top to get more from their wine. Does it make a difference? See the wine experiments at the end of this book.

It shouldn't be necessary to mention that a wineglass should be clean and odorless. But sometimes restaurants, in their zeal to make their glassware clean, use rinsing aids that leave behind a strong mineral smell. If you're spending a lot of money on a bottle of wine in a restaurant, sniff the empty glass first. At home, a film of grease can settle on a previously clean glass. It's no reflection on the quality of the housekeeping—cooking fats disperse in the air and settle on everything in a kitchen. An additional rinsing and a wipe with a clean towel are all you need.

> Unless you're trying to warm with your hand a wine that has been served a bit too cold, it is customary to hold and pass wineglasses by their stems.

The more complex and fragile the taste of the wine, the more important these niceties are. That's why we always have some simple, yummy, straightforward wine around for the times when you want something to drink and you'd like the preparations to be less complex than they would be for childbirth. Unless you have a character attracted to such things, you don't want to go through elaborate rituals every time you pop a cork. On the other hand, there are times that call for the extra care. We have feral days and feast days, and there's a place for wine in both.

Corks and Bottles

Cork in various forms

You may have noticed the central place of the cork in all of this ritual. Corks have been used to stopper wine bottles for at least 400 years because cork compresses easily to fit inside the neck of a bottle and then expands to keep air out and wine in. A proper cork will keep wine safe for twenty years or more. The problem is that a lot of corks aren't so proper any more.

Some corks harbor microbes that make the wonderfully named chemical, 2,4,6-trichloroanisole (TCA). TCA in contaminated corks leaches out into the wine, and it doesn't take much to ruin a bottle. Most of us can smell TCA at levels as low as 3 parts per trillion.

Industry sources now admit that up to 5 percent of bottles are contaminated. There are other problems with corks: Sometimes they simply fail to protect the wine from air. With more wine being produced every year and the supply of cork being relatively fixed, more cork of marginal quality is making it into wine bottles.

So what to do? Unfortunately, there's no synthetic material that can combine cork's compressibility and elasticity without being almost impossible to remove. For the moment, the best alternative is the screwcap or Stelvin® closure. They make a perfect seal, they can be opened without fuss, and there's evidence that they can last as long as the best corks.

Why, with such a high failure rate for cork, hasn't the industry simply switched over to screwcaps? There are a few technical considerations, but most of the answer lies in consumer resistance. For many older consumers, the screwcap meant cheap wine and the cork was a symbol of quality. As a new generation of wine drinkers comes along, look for the screwcap to capture a larger share of the market and the crackling sound of a twisted metal top to re-place the pop of a cork as part of the romance of wine.

In the meantime, there's a certain sadness to the transition. In a way, corks are what made fine wine possible. Before mass-produced bottles and corks to seal them, wine that traveled any great distance from its winery went in barrels. Barrels let in a small amount of air so spoilage began as soon as the wine left the winery. The consumer who couldn't buy his own barrel went to the wine shop with a pail or pitcher. In England, at least, he would have several grades to choose from but not much selection at any single price level. His wine would begin to go sour immediately.

With a distribution system like that, there wasn't much incentive to improve the quality of wine. Glass bottles promised to change all that: Glass was air-tight. The wine would keep, even improve with age. More importantly, it en-abled small quantities of wine to be distributed: You could buy a few bottles of this and a few more of that. Competition entered the modern wine trade in bottles.

Strong glass bottles came along in England in the 1660s. At first, they were stoppered with glass, each stopper being ground individually to fit its bottle and then tied in place. Uniform plugs of cork gradually replaced the custom-tailored glass. The cork, exported from Portugal, was inserted for half its length in the bottleneck, and the consumer twisted it out.

The corkscrew came along a few years later, at the end of the century, and corks could then be driven flush with the bottle's neck. Alas, the quality of cork has declined in the face of increasing demand, and some of the world's most interesting wines are now stopped with plugs made from cellu-lose fibers or plastic. The screw cap was developed in France in the 1960s by Pechiney and patented under the name of Stelvin. Many winemakers feel that this is by far the most effective closure in terms of protecting the wine, but consumers so far are resistant to them. It may depend on some-one developing a satisfying ritual for opening a bottle with a screw cap closure.

Corkscrews

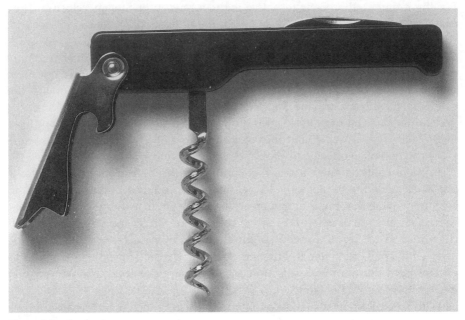

The waiter's corkscrew

We are a people with too much time on our hands, so it's not surprising that we have generated at least a hundred variations on the corkscrew.

The only thing that matters is this: The business end of a corkscrew, called the **worm,** should be a wire formed in a spiral (see illustration). Corkscrews with stamped worms that resemble wood screws should be rejected, shunned, even **anathematized.** Here's why. The wire displaces the least amount of cork and gives the greatest amount of lifting surface. The stamped worm drills a hole in the cork and offers only its edges for lift. If the cork is old or soft, this latter arrangement can leave you with a half a crumbled cork in the bottle.

Here's what the worm of a proper corkscrew looks like from the side: The wire is slim and makes a spiral that's wide enough to slip a paper match inside. The tip is pointed and sharp. That said, there are some variations in the way the worm is applied to the cork and in the means for applying the force that withdraws it. Two devices come highly recommended:

1. The Screwpull—This consists of two pieces. One sits on top of the bottleneck with a hole over the cork and two flexible legs that go down the side. You grab the legs and gently squeeze them around the bottle. The sec-

ond part is a worm that goes through the hole and into the cork. When the worm is screwed all the way into the cork, the cork rises up out of the bottle. The Screwpull is as close to foolproof as is possible and costs about $20.

2. The Waiter's Corkscrew—Five inches long and less than half an inch thick, this lovely little tool slips conveniently in the waiter's pocket (or your dop kit, glove compartment, or desk drawer). If you need a knife to cut the capsule around the top of the bottle, a non-lethal one unfolds in a second. Then you flip out the worm and turn it into the cork. When the worm is buried, flop the bottle-opener-like arm down so it rests on the lip of the bottle and lift the opposite side. The lever action removes the cork, although you may have to wiggle it out for the last few millimeters or so. This corkscrew is available in any kitchen supply store for about $5.

Discussion Questions

- What other aspects of everyday life involve rituals?
- Why do you think people are intimidated by ordering wine? What's so scary about fancy restaurants?
- Debate this: The best place to store wine is at the wine store until you need it.
- When might you put a bottle of red wine on ice?
- How much do you add to the cost of drinking wine by buying good glasses?
- When would it be really wise to pour wine from a bottle to another container for serving?
- What would you want to drink with an anchovy pizza? A fast-food burger? A bean burrito?
- Without using your hands, describe the shape of the worm of a proper corkscrew.

Glossary

capsule The molded cap that surrounds the cork and the top of the bottle. It used to be made of lead foil to discourage bugs, but corrosion under the capsule created lead salts that could end up in the wine. Today they are made of aluminum or plastic.

decanting Pouring a wine from its original bottle into another container before serving.

entrée In America, the main course.

ritual A repeated act with cultural meaning that conveys information and manipulates emotion.

worm The part of a corkscrew that is actually inserted in the cork.

Chapter **8**

Wine and Food and Commerce

When you finish this chapter, you will:

- *Have a sophisticated understanding of the relationship between food and wine.*
- *Be able to impress your friends and family with that understanding.*
- *Know some basic techniques for incorporating wine in your cooking.*
- *Understand the basic economics behind the cost of wine.*
- *Understand what makes wine more expensive in the restaurant than in the retail store.*
- *Be pleased to know that the market for wine isn't perfect and that some of its imperfections will allow you, as an educated consumer, to score an occasional bargain.*

If the wine ritual in a restaurant makes people nervous, the simple business of figuring out what wine to serve with dinner can make them near rigid with fright. It seems like very sophisticated business. (It can be very sophisticated indeed, but that doesn't make it intimidating or unpleasant at a simpler level. The same points could be made about shooting pool or making love.) They may have heard a lot of complicated talk about how wine x "goes with" beef and wine y "matches" grilled fish. They know they could memorize all the different combinations. (What wine goes with Buffalo Wings, anyway?)

Well, relax, there are a few things you should know that will give you all the self-confidence of an expert even if you don't know all the jargon.

- **There's a lot of disagreement about what "goes with" and "matches" mean.** Sometimes they mean that the wine contrasts pleasantly with some characteristic of the food. Sometimes the wine seems like a missing

Dinner and a glass of wine

ingredient, and sometimes it emphasizes some flavor in the food. The connection between the wine and the food isn't as tight as those expressions suggest. You don't pour the wine on your food; you take little sips in between bites. The dance is less like a waltz with dancers in each other's arms and more like a pas de deux where they share the same stage, sometimes touching, sometimes not.

Remember that wine <u>is</u> a food, and we don't fuss too much about whether the string beans go with the roast. Relax, this is supposed to be fun and remember, too, to act confident even if you're not.

- **It follows that it's hard to make a really bad match.** Usually, the worst thing that happens is that rich food overpowers a wimpy wine. Occasionally, a mismatched wine can diminish the flavor of your meal, but you'd still have to work hard to come up with a real stinker. Most of the time, if you make a "mistake" and you make it with confidence, you'll just seem a little eccentric in your tastes—like Tom Wolfe and Mark Twain in their white suits.
- **The most reliable rule is that big wines go with big food, delicate wines with lighter food.** You already know the difference. Big food is chewy, aromatic, or spicy: It's beef stew or cassoulet, but it's also a crab cake with Old Bay or anything from the grill. Big wine is full-bodied, aromatic, and spicy with a long finish, and it's usually red.

Lighter food is mostly fish, fruit, anything with a cream sauce, or a sweet glaze. Light food with a substantial sauce becomes big food. Delicate wine is acidic, fruity, and floral, and it's often white, but sometimes it's light-bodied or fresh-tasting red. Pinot Noir is an example of the former, Beaujolais of the latter. A few foods straddle the borderline: barbecued ribs, roast chicken, baked lasagna, foie gras. They allow you to emphasize the food by picking a delicate wine or submerge it slightly with a heartier one.

- **If a wine leaves your mouth watering, it's probably going to be better with food than a wine that doesn't.** We salivate when we're hungry. We even use the watering mouth as a figure of speech for intense desire. The system works the other way too: When our mouths water, we feel hunger. The easiest, most natural food/wine pairings happen with wines whose acid or tannin leave you (politely) drooling.
- **It's almost impossible to make a good pairing if the food or wine is at an extreme temperature.**

Cooking with Wine

Wine used in cooking adds richness and depth of flavor and an acidity that provides some sparkle to other flavors. The wine that you use for cooking should be drinkable; that is, it should have no vinegary or other off flavors. It does not have to be of the same quality as the wine you serve at dinner, although it makes sense to select the same general type for both the cooking pot and the table.

When you cook with wine, you boil away the alcohol and destroy or disperse most of the subtle flavors. (see Wine Experiment 2.) That's why using great wine in the pot is wasteful and unnecessary. On the other hand, foul smells and sour tastes are concentrated by cooking, so pour that bottle of soured red wine down the drain.

Because wine's subtleties die in the heat, it also makes sense to use a wine with a pronounced character. Cooked Pinot Noir or Chardonnay have only a little to offer a dish; stronger varieties like Gewurztraminer and Moscato are more to the point, as are big reds like Cabernet Sauvignon and Zinfandel and the richly patterned fortified wines like madeira, sherry, and port.

Except in a few rare dessert preparations, wine in cooking should cook long enough to reduce its volume by one half or more. That means that wine added to an already existent sauce should cook for at least five minutes before being served. The alcohol in raw wine is as much a distraction on the plate as it is a necessity in the glass. Reduced wine can be made separately and stored in a tightly stoppered bottle in the refrigerator or frozen in ice cube trays for portion-controlled use later on. See the recipe below.

- Wine is one of the classic marinades, and everyone who plays with food has to go through a period where no piece of meat is allowed to escape the kitchen unmarinated. Marinades often reduce the food they're bathing to mere mush, so be judicious.

- There are two schools of thought on the use of wine in risotto. The first school insists on using a red wine mixed with stock throughout the cooking. The second school says that a large quantity of champagne should be used at the beginning of cooking and a small amount at the end. They're both right.

- Contrary to everything else stated here, a small amount of uncooked wine can be sprinkled on roasted meat or used in a vinaigrette dressing. Raw wine is also appropriate if it is sweetened and used as a part of dessert. The sugar reduces the spirituous quality of the wine and emphasizes the fruit.

- If you own an ice cream machine, try freezing some sweetened or concentrated wine and serving it as a sorbet between courses. Add a sprig of herb to the wine if you cook it down. See the note on reduction sauces below.

- If you use wine to deglaze a saute pan, let the resulting liquid return to the gentle boil and taste until any harshness is gone. Sherry can stand to cook a bit longer, and as it does, it develops some extra complexity.

- Snapper soup benefits from a dollop of sherry at the end, and port or Madeira are wonderful finishes to many stews. Of course, you'll observe the caution above and not use any wine that deserves to go directly into the glass and thence into you.

- Steamed mussels can be cooked over wine instead of water, with a finely chopped onion or court bouillon added. This liquid can be gently reduced and suitably augmented to form a dipping sauce for the mussels. If you have any mussel broth/court bouillon/reduced wine mixture left over, it's freezable and makes a perfect poaching liquid for fish.

- If you find yourself with a quantity of red wine left over, you might try a reduction sauce. Reduction sauces are made by cooking the water out of some liquid, "reducing" its volume and concentrating its flavor. A red wine reduction sauce can be used straight up or be added to pan juices from a roast. You can also pour the almost finished sauce in the skillet in which you just sautéed something, scrape the bottom of the pan to dissolve the brownings, and pour the result over the just-cooked food.

> In a pinch, a couple tablespoons of raw wine can be poured into the just emptied skillet, the heat raised and the bubbling wine stirred to dissolve the pan brownings. The resulting liquid can be thickened or poured over food as-is. This is called deglazing the pan and it not only adds some wine to your dish, it saves all the wonderful browned tastes that otherwise might have gone down the drain when the pan was washed.

Sweat a few tablespoons of onion and a clove of garlic (chopped) in a little bit of olive oil. If you have celery or carrot handy, a little bit of that adds complexity to the finished sauce. When the onion is softened, add some chopped tomato or a spoonful of tomato paste, black pepper, and a little balsalmic vinegar. If you've got some sherry or port around, add a teaspoon or so.

Pour in the remains of the wine. If you have an herb handy that you think would be good, add it now. Cook the mixture slowly until you've lost about half the volume. Skim the top from time to time. When it looks like there's a lot of vegetables in the pan in relation to the amount of wine, strain them out. You don't want to scorch the vegetables and add a burned taste to the sauce.

Return the wine to the pan and cook some more. You'll reduce it until it looks like a sauce to you and then taste for salt. Half a bottle yields about two to three ounces of finished sauce.

- Sweet wines can be incorporated in whipped creams or gelatins for dessert and used as a topping for fruit or lightly sweetened cakes. Fruits soaked or poached in wine and dried fruits rehydrated in an appropriate wine are simple and elegant conclusions to a meal.

In a Restaurant

Have a glass while perusing the menu

We began this chapter imagining you in a restaurant choosing a wine from the wine list, so let's consider for a moment what that wine will cost you. If you have spent some time in the wine store, you may have worked up a pretty fair idea of retail prices. You certainly know the cost of some of your favorites, and you may be aware of the prices just above and below your customary range.

So when the wine list came your way, you may have been surprised to find that the prices were much higher than what you were used to. You are comfortable with the fact that the restaurant has to charge you more for the steak than it paid for it. After all, it costs money to build a kitchen and even more to run it. There's also spoilage and the rent on kitchen floor space to consider. Besides, you may feel that the chef and his staff bring some skill, perhaps even some wisdom, to the task of selecting and preparing your food and you're more than happy to pay for that.

But the wine seems somehow different. You just saw a bottle in the wine shop next door for $15, and here it is on the menu for $52. It seems outrageous.

In fact, if you are ordering the same wine that you see on the shelf, a markup of 346 percent is pretty steep, but by no means the highest markup that you will encounter. But before you summon the manager, call him a cad and a bounder, and challenge him to a duel, there are a few things you might want to consider.

- It costs employee time to buy, store, account for, and sell the wine.
- Proper wine storage is expensive (see Chapter 7).
- The restaurant has to pay for its wine before it sells it, so scarce capital is tied up in the wine room. Most restaurants can take at least thirty days to pay for their food, but most states prohibit extension of credit for wine.

If the wine isn't a common item in your local store and had to be specially ordered, there are other things to consider.

- Specially ordered wine often has to be paid for before it's delivered, which ties up money for longer periods of time.
- If the wine requires aging or sells slowly, the cost of buying it increases.
- Shipping costs may be much higher.
- The same considerations of time, taste, and skill that apply to fine food also apply to the selection of fine wine.
- You're more likely to encounter special wines in places where the overhead, and therefore the markup on everything, is already high.

So what's reasonable? For an average, high-volume bottle of wine in a low-overhead bistro, twice the retail or a bit more is fine. Expect to pay triple for special wine or wine in special places. When the margin goes much higher, see if you can find a reason to justify it. If you can't, you might consider ordering wine by the glass.

Afterword:
Continuing Your Wine Education

Congratulations. You've completed a college course in wine. I think I can say, with a certainty that professors in most other subjects would envy, that you probably want to learn more. Here are some suggestions for continuing your wine education:

- **Taste**—Use the wine experiments in the next section as a start; then use every opportunity to taste some more. Sometimes it's worthwhile, with a field as cluttered and complex as wine, to impose some system on your explorations just so you can remember what you're doing.

  You may even want to specialize maniacally for a while. I can't overstate the value of concentrating on one particular type of wine for a fixed period. Take a springtime to drink Chianti or a winter for Zinfandel. Nothing sharpens the perceptions like paying attention to the differences between close relations.
- **Read**—Books are good for the big picture; remember that a professional is someone who understands the context of his or her subject, so reading about wine history, winemaking, and the wine trade is not a waste of time. Read magazines, too. *The Wine Spectator, The Wine Advocate,* and *Wine and Spirits* are all good. There are occasional good pieces in the cooking magazines, *The New York Times,* and *The Philadelphia Inquirer. The Wall Street Journal* does some of its best work in its weekly wine column. Everybody should have a wine atlas to help visualize the land that the wine comes from. I use Oz Clarke's *World Atlas of Wine.*

  There's a way in which even ordinary books on subjects you care about become extraordinarily good reads, so read voraciously. You may even find that reading goes well with a glass of wine.
- **Dine**—Include wine in your meals when you can. Give some thought to matching or contrasting wine and food and pay attention to how things taste.

- **Visit**—Most vineyards welcome the public and provide tastings free or for a small fee. When you can, make those visits in France, Italy, and California. Until then, there are wineries in every state in the union and many Canadian provinces. Go in a crowd and go with a designated driver.
- **Taste (again)**—Get together with a few friends and have your own tasting. The purpose of a tasting, by the way, is comparison and evaluation. If you assemble, let's say, four bottles of wine and seven friends, each person can have a three-ounce taste of each of the wines and no one has to load up with alcohol or break the budget to do it. A good way to do this is to pick four wines from the same grape and in the same price range. There is a tremendous virtue to tasting things in groups.

  (Several wines tasted together are called a "flight.")
- **Ask**—Question your faculty, your co-op supervisors, and anyone else. Ask for recommendations and advice, none of which you should take too seriously. Try some weird combinations; be original.
- **Create**—Make up an appetizer, a soup, a fish, fowl, or meat dish that uses wine as a principal ingredient.
- **Be perverse**—Find a wine you like and admire. Then try to pair it with food that is both delicious in itself and hostile to the taste of the wine. In other words, deliberately seek out a bad food and wine combination.
- **Specialize**—Pick a grape or a region and taste as many examples of wine of that sort as you can. Try to taste them with as little distraction as possible; lay off the Chardonnay, for instance, in the month in which you're doing Zinfandel.
- **Find a Teacher**—There are lots of private wine schools and structured tasting programs available these days. When you start out with a teacher or school, look for teachers who know how to share their knowledge. Communication skills are more important than tasting skills. After a while, as you become more certain, you will want a teacher who can share his or her own uncertainties, questions, and puzzlements.
- **Celebrate**—A man I know takes a bottle of champagne, a friend, and a couple of juice glasses to the top of the Philadelphia Art Museum steps around dusk . . . he does not imitate Rocky. Instead he follows the tasting ritual in Chapter 2.

Wine Experiments

Prologue

You may want to return to Chapter 2 and review the notes on tasting, but at the least, follow this protocol.

- Eliminate distractions and concentrate on the wine.
- Swirl the wine in the glass to increase evaporation and release the bouquet.
- Use your nose to take sharp, deep sniffs before you drink.
- Swish the wine around in your mouth to get the maximum contact between it and your tongue, and also to increase your sense of the bouquet.
- With your mouth full, part your lips a little and draw some air over the wine.
- Swallow or spit as circumstances dictate.
- Pay attention to the aftertaste, or finish.

Be sure to notice the color of the wine, too. Hold your glass up to the light and inspect the thin line of liquid where the wine meets the side of the glass. A purplish red suggests a young, raw wine; anything with a hint of orange is probably overaged.

Tasting Sheets

A tasting sheet has two purposes. First, it helps you keep track of which glass has which wine. It's astonishingly easy to get confused when there are two wines in question, thirty-two times easier when there are four, and so on. I feel strongly that when you're engaged in deep contemplation and phenomenological experimentation, you should not have to stop to wonder where you left the Chateau Margaux or the Chaddsford Pinot Noir.

The sheet's other purpose is to serve as a repository for notes. It's easy to forget, especially if you're tasting a lot of different wines, just what you liked or disliked about this or that. Notes are the answer, and I always distribute sheets prepunched to make them convenient to file in a binder.

Wine Experiment 1

Purpose: To identify the characteristic taste of a young red wine and to learn the effects of decanting (aerating) on that taste.

You'll need two bottles of Cabernet Sauvignon of recent vintage, which should be enough for six to eight people.

Open one bottle and pour the wine into another bottle, a pitcher, or a wine decanter. Pour straight down the center with a lot of splashing. Place the decanted wine and the unopened bottle in a cool place and allow them both to reach drinking temperature.

After two hours, open the second bottle. Pour three ounces of the newly opened wine for each taster and put it in place 1 on your tasting sheet. Pour three ounces of the decanted wine and put it in place 2. Compare the bouquets *before* you begin tasting.

Describe the bouquet of each sample. In this case, you'll also probably notice a difference in strength or freshness of the bouquet. Then describe the mouth feel or body of the wine. Does it feel rich and thick or thin and watery? Is there any astringency? Do you notice any secondary flavors? Does the finish seem to last a long time or does it disappear quickly?

Wine Experiment 2

Purpose: To identify the taste of wine as an ingredient in cooked food.

You will need one bottle of wine that might be used in cooking. Since we have started with Cabernets, we might as well stick with them. Open a bottle and pour eight ounces of wine into a nonreactive saucepan. Bring the wine to a simmer and reduce to four ounces. Allow this to cool and pour an ounce in a glass in place 1. Pour some of the uncooked wine in a glass in place 2.

In most tastings, you look for the differences between wines; in this case, you want to find the similarities. To what extent can you recognize the characteristics of the wine in glass 2 when you taste the reduced wine? After you have tasted both glasses and reflected on the nature and alchemy of transformation, you'll have three ounces of not very drinkable red stuff and a half a bottle of wine. This calls for dinner.

At the simplest, you might want to begin with a broth or vegetable soup and add an ounce of the wine to it, tasting both before and after. Next, you might brown a hamburger, turkey burger, chicken breast, or lamb chop and deglaze the pan with another ounce. If you're having pasta, an ounce in your tomato sauce would be good, and if you're having stew, that little ounce makes a difference. Before you add the wine, you have mere stew. An ounce later and you have a dish to move mountains, a convocation of gifts from the earth and the labor of man, a hymn to fertility, and a goad to philosophy.

If there's an ounce left over, you could use it for salad dressing or dribble it on your pie. You could pour it in the center of an about-to-be-baked apple or a just recently baked potato or yam.

Wine Experiment 3

Purpose: To compare two different wines and make an evaluation. If you're quite intrigued by this Cabernet thing, you might get two similarly priced bottles for this experiment. If you have had enough Cabernet, Zinfandel is an excellent candidate.

You're going to repeat the same procedure you did in Experiment 1 with each of these bottles, putting the decanted wines on the right side of your tasting sheet and the corresponding just-opened wines to their left. It's easy to get confused here, so fill glasses from one decanter and place them all on the tasting sheets. Then fill glasses from the just-opened bottle of the same wine. Repeat these steps with the next wine; first the decanted, then the just-opened.

You will be trying to handle two variables here, so your tasting should proceed slowly. Take time between tastes to have a cracker or a glass of water. By the way, if you're concerned about limiting your alcohol intake, this is the time to learn the wine taster's trick. You can get almost all of the sensation that the wine has to offer without swallowing it, and it's good form and even wise to discreetly spit the wine back into the glass or into a spitoon provided for the purpose. This is how it's possible to taste thirty wines before lunch and still be standing up when lunch is served.

Wine Experiment 4

Purpose: To see if the glass you use really has any effect on the taste of the wine. Assemble some tumblers of various heights, a brandy snifter, a dish-shaped champagne glass, a champagne flute, and a traditional-stemmed wine glass. Measure identical amounts of wine, three ounces for example, and pour into each glass. Wait a minute or two and then sniff the bouquet from each glass. Does it seem more pronounced from any particular one?

If one of the glasses seems to nurture a more profound bouquet, wait a few minutes and repeat the experiment. This time, sniff the most productive glass after you have tried all the others. If it still promotes the bouquet more than the others, you can be sure that the shape is the difference.

Now take a taste from each of the glasses. Was there a clear-cut winner? If there was, why wouldn't you use that glass for all the cold beverages that you drink? If you're a relentlessly scientific type, you might try this experiment with both a cheap wine and a more expensive one. You could continue on, sampling reds and whites, sweet wines and dry.

Glossary

Acetic Acid   Otherwise known as vinegar. There's a little bit of it naturally in all wine, but in excess it makes you think of salad dressing.

Acid   A naturally occurring compound having a sour taste and capable of neutralizing an alkali. Fermented grapes produce a variety of acids and wine generally is about ½% acid by weight.

Alcohol   (specifically ethyl alcohol) A colorless, flammable liquid with a faintly sweet taste that is produced by the fermentation of sugars.

Alcoholism   The continued and abusive use of alcohol.

Analgesic   A substance that deadens pain.

Anthocyanins   The bluish pigment tannins that make new red wine look purple

Anthropology   The science of everything human. As with most studies that claim to be about everything, it eventually came to be about nothing.

A.O.C   Appellation D'Origine Contrôllée on a French wine label means that the wine is authentic—that it comes from the region named on the bottle. It is not a guarantee of quality.

Appellation   Informally, any named wine making region.

Appellation Law   The rules that allow a winery to use the name of a region on its labels.

Astringency   Having the property of contracting the tissues or canals of the body: puckery.

Auslese   German for 'selected.' Its use means that the grapes are extra ripe.

Barrel Fermented   The wine has been fermented in a small oak barrel to impart a creamy texture and taste. When overdone, barrel fermented wines lose their fruit.

Barrique   Oak barrel holding 24 cases; wine stored in barriques picks up flavor from the wood and also from the small amounts of air that infiltrate the barrel. Originally used in France, barriques nowadays are employed all around the winemaking world.

Beerenauslese   Very sweet German wines. Made from grapes infected with noble rot (*see* Botrytis Cinerea).

Blush   A distinctly American word for a pink wine made from red grapes. The pale color comes from the wine being in contact with the skins for only a short period of time.

Body   The feeling of thickness that a wine has in your mouth. Thick- or full-bodied wines may remind you of the feeling of cream. Light- or thin-bodied wines feel more like water. Remember, in wine, the sensation of body comes from alcohol, the solids dissolved or suspended in the wine, and the unfermented sugar (if any).

Botrytis Cinerea   The ashy-grey fungus that can infect grapes at harvest time, also called Noble Rot. Botrytis takes moisture from the grapes which increases the concentration of sugar.

Bouquet   Some authorities claim that bouquet refers to that part of the wine's smell that is attributable to wine-making practices, while 'aroma' means those smells that have survived intact from the grape. Current usage, however, seems to favor 'bouquet' as meaning all the smells floating from the glass up to your nose.

Carbonated   Containing small amounts of dissolved carbon dioxide gas.

Carbonic Maceration   A kind of fermentation in which crushed grapes begin to ferment inside their own skins. The result is a fresh, fruity wine that is drinkable immediately but doesn't age well.

Capsule   The molded cap that surrounds the cork and the top of the bottle. It used to be made of lead foil to discourage bugs, but corrosion under the capsule created lead salts that could end up in the wine. Today they are made of aluminum or plastic.

Centrifuged   Spun in a tank to separate the solid from the liquid portion of new wine.

Chaptalization   The addition of sugar or concentrated grape juice to *must* in order to increase alcohol.

Charmat   The bulk method for making sparkling wine. The second fermentation happens in a big, closed tank, kind of like a soda bottle. Charmat sparkling wines are a lot cheaper but never as good as the ones made by *method champenoise.*

Château   In Bordeaux, France, both the building where wine is made and the vineyards around it. The words are rarely used in other parts of France, but have been picked up enthusiastically in America and Australia (*see* Domaine).

Clone   When wine people talk about a clone, they're usually referring to a population of plants that have all been cloned from a single individual. These clones are selected by growers for their ability to make better wine in a particular vineyard.

Clos   A vineyard enclosed by a stone wall. Originally used in Burgundy, the term has been borrowed freely (and loosely) in the United States.

Communion   An act of ritual sharing of food and drink.

Continuum   Something in which a common character is discernible and distinctions can only be made by reference to small distinctions of quantity.

Corked   Refers to wines that have picked up a stink due to a defective cork. The smell is intense, reminiscent of wet dirt. If you get a corked bottle of wine, return it to the store and get your money back. Honest retailers know there is some corked wine in the marketplace.

Cremant French term for sparkling wines made outside Champagne. Cremant wines are usually less fizzy (and less expensive) than Champagne.

Cru On a French wine label refers to a ranking, 1er cru means first rank., etc.

Crusades Any of a series of ultimately futile wars waged by infidels in the 11th thru 13th centuries in an attempt to take control of the Biblical land of Israel from the heathens.

Decanting Pouring a wine from its original bottle into another container before serving.

D.O. Denominaciòn d'Origen on a Spanish wine label means that the wine is authentic and it comes from the region named on the bottle. It is not a guarantee of quality.

D.O.C. Denominazione d'Origine Controllata on an Italian wine label means that the wine is authentic—that it comes from the region named on the bottle. It is not a guarantee of quality.

Domaine The equivalent, in Burgundy, of Château in Bordeaux. The term has been borrowed in the new world to make you think Burgundian thoughts about, and pay Burgundian prices for, new world wine.

Dry "Completely without sugar." Dry wines are those where all the sugar has been converted by fermentation into alcohol.

Enology The fancy word for the study of wines and winemaking—also spelled oenology.

Enophile A wine lover. While it takes years to become an enologist, you can become an enophile just by reading this book.

Esters Chemicals formed by the reaction between the newly developing alcohol and the natural acids in grape juice. There are dozens of esters that appear in wine and they are a main source of flavor and aroma.

Ethyl Acetate Formed by acetic acid bacteria. This is the smell you got from that bottle that was left out on the counter overnight.

Entrée In America, the main course.

Ferment To convert sugar into alcohol through the action of yeast.

Fermentation In this book, it mostly refers to sugar in grape juice being consumed by yeast, producing alcohol, heat, and carbon dioxide. Also called alcoholic fermentation to distinguish it from malolactic fermentation.

Filtration Clarifying wine by passing it through a screen. Some screens are small enough to remove particles as small as bacteria and yeast cells.

Fining Tthe clarification of wine by adding a substance which sinks through the wine pulling fine particles out.

Finish The sensation a wine leaves in your mouth after you've swallowed it.

Free-run Juice that's produced by the grapes at the top of the crushing vat, pressing on the grapes below. Some vineyards believe that this is the best juice and sometimes brag about it on their labels.

Late Harvest Grapes that are allowed to remain on the vine for longer than usual. Some of the extra sugar that they accumulate stays behind when the yeast is exhausted, so these words on a label indicate a sweet wine.

Lees The sludge of yeast and grape solids that settles to the bottom of the wine after fermentation. A wine sitting on its lees gains complexity of flavor but runs the risk of infection.

Maceration Period of time that skins are in contact with the juice. If you think of a teabag, you know that longer soak in hot water makes for darker tea. In the same way, long macerations make for more color and flavor in the wine.

Malolactic Fermentation The conversion of sour malic acid into softer lactic acid. This fermentation is done by bacteria after the first (alcoholic) fermentation is complete. It's encouraged in most red wine and in some whites.

Malt Sprouted grains of barley whose starch is ready to be converted into sugar.

Must Pressed grape juice that hasn't turned fully into wine.

Nouveau 'New' in French; refers to new wine like Beaujolais that's available to drink by November in the year of harvest.

NV Non-vintage. A wine without a declared year of vintage, possibly blended from wines of more than one year.

Olfactory Epithelium The dime-sized patch of tissue in your skull where the receptors for your sense of smell are located.

Opulent Rich, abundant, thickly textured.

Otiose Weak or distant.

Pasteurization The heating of wine to kill most bacteria and yeast. Pasteurized wines are more stable, but there's a lot of flavor lost in the process. Usually only done to the cheapest wines.

Pectin A gummy carbohydrate found in fruits, particularly in their skins. It accounts for the cloudy nature of most fruit juices and is used to make jellies.

Petillant From the French, it means lightly sparkling. It's usually said of a wine that's refermented a little in the bottle with the CO_2 being trapped and dissolved in the wine.

Plonk Ordinary, boring, one-dimensional wine, grape juice with alcohol.

Pomace Is the stuff left over after the crushed grapes are pressed and the juice run off—mostly stems and skins. Pomace can be flooded with water and a small amount of harsh juice recovered. This can be fermented and then distilled to make drinks like grappa. *Also called* vinaccia.

Potable Drinkable.

Prohibition The 13-year period from 1920 to 1933 in which no wine could be sold legally in the United States. By extension, any such rule.

Racking Moving the wine off its lees, usually from one barrel to another.

Ratings Attempts to summarize the complexity of a wine's taste and all the possible individual responses to it in a single number. For a value-based alternative to ratings, consult http://shortcourseinwine.blogspot.com.

Ritual A repeated act with cultural meaning that conveys information and manipulates emotion.

Reserve Used on a label to suggest higher quality than the normal plonk the winery turns out. In the United States it has no legal meaning and may be used just as a marketing ploy. In Italy and Spain (riserva and reserva) it's strictly defined and means that the wine has been aged for a longer period than the minimum for the type.

Residual Sugar(s) The amount of sugar left in a wine after fermentation is complete. Perfectly dry wines have no rs; small amounts contribute to the body of the wine, and, at amounts over 1%, almost everyone notices sweetness.

Rosé A wine made from red grapes that was not allowed to sit on its skins long enough to pick up color during maceration. Less often, a blend of red and white wines. Rosés are lighter in flavor than reds and sometimes chosen for summertime drinking.

Sacrament A ceremony usually involving some physical manifestation of an obligation or vow undertaken by the participant.

Salutary Favorable to good health.

Second Label Some very good wineries will have some grapes that aren't up to their standards. Rather than dilute the value of their brand name, they are more likely to bottle the wine under another name. Second labels are sometimes very good values.

Soccer Riots An extension of the sport of European football in which crowds of supporters of one team battle with fans of another. As recently as 1985, 39 people died in a battle at the Heysel pitch and 96 were trampled or crushed to death in riots at Hillsborough.

Sparkling Wine Nowadays, only wine from Champagne can be called by that name, so this is the common term for any wine with bubbles. Italian sparkling wines are labeled 'spumante,' Spanish ones are called 'cava.'

Spritzy Having a small amount of carbonation. Spritzy wines may have a pronounced bubbly mouth feel or just a small tang. If a wine becomes less acidic after it's been opened for a few minutes, that's attributable to spritziness.

Structural Harmony In red wines, a balance between alcohol and sugar on one hand and tanni and acid on the other. In whites, it's simply acid balanced with sugar and alcohol.

Table Wine As opposed to fortified or dessert wine, has 8 to 15% alcohol, the implication being that this is the wine that you have with dinner. On a wine label, especially in French (vin du table) or Italian (vino da tavola) it announces that the wine wasn't made in accordance with any particular appellation law.

Tannin A family of soluble compounds that act as astringents and antiseptics. Found in the leaves and bark of plants, tannins are also used to cure leather and treat wounds.

Terroir All of the factors, soil, topography, and climate that make one place different from another. European winemakers who have vineyards that make great wine often credit their particular 'terroir.'

Thirty Years' War A series of particularly savage, religiously inflamed wars that resulted in widespread destruction in Europe between 1618 and 1648. Estimates of civilian deaths range from 15% to 30% of the total population.

Ubiquitous Present everywhere. Of course, this 'everywhere' is used in a special sense. If something were truly everywhere, then there would be nothing else in the universe. And that's not true, even of yeast.

Ullage The empty space between the cork and the wine in a bottle. If that space is larger than normal (about an inch) it probably means that wine has leaked out past a faulty cork.

Varietal A wine made mostly from a single grape variety. In the United States, a wine must contain 75% of the variety named on the label.

Varieties Named, genetically distinct populations of grape vines: Barbera, Blaufrankisch, Brunello, etc.

Vin de garde Wine intended to be stored for some time before it's drunk.

Vintner A person who makes or sells wine. *"What does the vintner buy that's half so precious as what he sells?"*—Omar Khayyam, the Rubiyat.

Vinous A vague, unspecific, wine-like character.

Wine Fermented fruit juice. In some wine courses, a final exam question asks for a definition of wine that is both more frivolous and more true than 'fermented fruit juice.' Here's one such definition from Ambrose Bierce's *The Devil's Dictionary:* Fermented grape-juice known to the Women's Christian Union as "liquor," sometimes as "rum." "Wine, madam, is God's next best gift to man."

Worm The part of a corkscrew that is actually inserted in the cork.

Index

spittoons, 22, 123
squash, 1
stabilization, 85, 96
sugars, 1, 2, 6, 25, 27, 32, 33, 45, 55, 71, 82, 86, 87, 88, 92, 97
sulphur dioxide, 4, 80
surface tension, 18
süssreserve, 92
Syrah/Shiraz, 75, 78

tannins, 22, 27, 32, 33, 48, 68, 69, 73, 91, 95, 103, 105
tartaric acid, 2, 19
taste buds, 21
tasting, 17–18, 24, 29
    blind, 24
    See also wine tastings
tawnies, 53
tea, 1
tears, 18. *See also* legs
temperature-sensitive patch, 106
terroir, 3, 83
Thirty Years' War, 96
threshold, 23
Thunderbird, 24
tirosh, 48
tomatoes, 1
Trebbiano, 56
trocken, 82
Twain, Mark, 114
2,4,6-trichloroanisole (TCA), 108

Valdobbiadene, 52
vanillin, 60
Vikings, 52
vinegar, 35
vines, See grape vines
vineyards, 3, 43, 59, 62, 72, 87–89, 95, 97, 120
vintners, 3, 24, 33
    California, 43
Vitis vinifera, 67
Volstead Act, 42
Vougeot, 76

Wachau Valley, 82
wallflowers, 1
water molecules, 18
whiskies, 40
Willamette Valley, 81
Wine Advocate, The, 119
Wine and Spirits, 29, 57, 119
wine casks, 60

wine education industry, 4
wineglasses, 107, 123
wine industry, 4
winemakers, 1, 3, 6, 7, 43, 49, 56, 68, 74, 75, 82, 83, 85, 86, 87, 88, 93, 95, 96
    American, 80
    and cost, 64
    German, 81–82
    supply for, 1
winemaking equipment, 4
winemaking techniques, 4, 48
wines
    aging, 99, 103
    as antiseptic, 14
    aromas, 17, 18, 19, 21, 23, 31, 33
    for awareness, 15
    barrels, 60, 61, 69, 80, 85, 93–94, 95, 98
    bottles, 61
    body, 22, 32
    bouquet, 19, 21, 22, 26, 32, 33, 121–22
    color, 19
    compound, 2
    containers, 59
    in cooking, 113, 115–17
    definition of, 1
    dry, 25, 54–55
    finish, 23
    for health, 15
    jars, 59
    relationship with civilization, 9
    and religion, 9
    and restaurant prices, 118
    role in culture, 9
    sparkling, 47, 50–52
    sweet, 54–55
    woodiness of, 66
Wine Spectator, The, 29, 57, 119
winestone potassium bitartarate, 19
wine tastings, 7
wine writer, 4, 31
Wolfe, Tom, 114

yarrow, 1
yeasts, 4, 5, 35, 45, 55, 85, 86, 87, 97
    airborne, 36, 86
    definition of, 1
    varieties of, 87
    wild, 1
    wine, 1

Zinfandel, 2, 7, 24, 49, 78–79, 83, 89, 115, 119, 122
zinnias, 1